Pushers of the Possible

MarketAPeel Agency
Vancouver, British Columbia, Canada

www.marketapeel.agency

Pushers of the Possible

Printed by Amazon's Global Print on Demand Services. 2019

MarketAPeel
411 939 Homer Street
Vancouver, BC
V6B 2W6

778-839-0521

ISBN: 9781097321001

Cover Design by Shannon Peel
Inside formatting by Shannon Peel

Icons made by smashicon from www.flaticon.com

Table of Contents

Author: Anthony C. Gruppo Sr
                                    CEO Marsh Commercial UK

Publisher   MarketAPeel Agency
Production Editor: Shannon Peel

Contributor and   Nina C. Helms
Sr. Editor:

Podcast Interviewees: Gene Waddy
                                   Jennifer Walsh
                                   Barry Beck
                                   Hakika Dubose-Wise
                                   Steve Maneri
                                   Ainsley Karas

Pushers of the Possible

What You Will Find

Inside the pages of this book you will find Anthony Gruppo interviewing other leaders on his Roots of Leadership Podcast to discover how they Pushed their Possible. After each interview he will explore the concepts raised by his guests to unpack those ideas and highlight how they can help you to reach your Possible. To truly assist you in finding your passion and formulating your goals are Anthony's inspiring quotes, thought provoking exercises and questions to help you explore the concepts for yourself.

Revealed in the interviews in the pages of this book you will learn that no matter where people start in life, where they end up is dependent on their own actions, attitudes and support systems. From their stories, the hope is you will find inspiration to Push the Possible in your life while becoming a servant leader to those around you. Keep a pen handy because this book will become a living document for your journey toward reaching your full potential.

Start your journey.

Getting paid to do something we are passionate about is a dream many people never realize because they do not push toward what is possible. When you are passionate about your career or business, opportunities come to you or reveal themselves because your attitude and energy changes. With passion you find yourself excited and anticipating each day. This is what Pushing the Possible means. It is about having a dream, a big dream, a dream you are passionate about.

You are a ship, loaded with your talent and genius, sailing on a journey to greatness. This book will help you to take control of the rudder and steer toward the Possible by sharing Pushers of the Possible stories. We cannot guarantee it will be smooth sailing as life rarely ever is. What we can guarantee is that you will read about and be inspired by business leaders who were told they would never make it, and instead of listening to the "naysayers" in their lives, pushed on toward the Possible and built something amazing. You are a Pusher of the Possible because you have faced adversity and overcome it. This means you have the mindset of an overachiever who shows up, does his/her best, discovers their passion and keeps achieving and breaking barriers.

The first step toward your Possible is to dream, to let your imagination fly, and thereby discover what you truly want. Do you want to disrupt your industry? Innovate a new way of doing something? Maybe you want to grow your business into a national or international powerhouse? Perhaps, you want to climb the corporate ladder to the top or be the best in the role you choose. Whatever your Possible is, we hope the stories from the Roots of Leadership Podcast inspire you to push toward it.....

Your Dream

In the future, when you are coming to the end of your time here on earth, what do you want to have accomplished?

Take some time to imagine a life beyond your wildest dreams. What does that life look like? Do this exercise or journal about this before you start reading the book to help you focus upon your Possible.

What is 'The Roots of Leadership?'

The Roots of Leadership Podcast is a platform for conversations with real people who started with little and fought to build something bigger than themselves. Each podcast is filled with ideas to help listeners improve both personally and professionally.

Anthony's guests are Pushers of the Possible because they were told they could NOT do something and went on to do it anyway, or in most cases, surpass their original dreams. You will find some of these interviews in the pages of this book, along with Anthony's thoughts to help you Push to your Possible.

Anthony On Roots of Leadership

I started interviewing CEOs and other servant leaders on the Roots of Leadership Podcast because I am fortunate to have access to amazing people. I wanted to give them a channel to the world to share their inspirational stories with young people, entrepreneurs, and other business leaders.

I also wanted to know more about these people, where they came from, how they grew up, how they got to where they are, and how they are committed to being a servant leader. The podcast achieves all of these intents and more.

The Roots of Leadership Podcast is popular because I have an incredible team of colleagues supporting me to create a high-quality show that benefits the audience, it is not about Anthony Gruppo. The Roots of Leadership is an easily accessible, welcoming platform where accomplished guests share inspirational and motivational stories. As the podcast grew in popularity, it evolved into a grassroots movement to find Pushers of the Possible in and around New York from audience members submitting names of guests they wanted to hear about.

The CEO Title

When I think about the title CEO, I see someone who can Coach themselves and others, be Entrepreneurial in their thinking, and act like an Owner, while asking others to see themselves in the same manner. I have often said the title CEO trips people up because they classify Chief Executive Officers as an elite group. The thing is, CEO is just a title, roles and responsibilities, and a mindset. It's not to be mistaken for who you are. Your title does not define you, so do not let it limit you. Push beyond the constraints of your job description, chose to be the CEO of your life, and as a CEO, build something bigger than yourself.

If you want to be a CEO, it takes commitment along every part of your career path. You must be willing to be in a constant state of change, ready to take on any challenge presented to you and come up with creative solutions to problems. It's important for your focus to be helping others, also known as servant leadership.

Outstanding effort is required to put the needs of others ahead of your growth or ego. It is about waking up and thinking, "How can I serve those whom I lead today?," instead of asking, "How will I be served by others?," or, "How can I be safe today?"

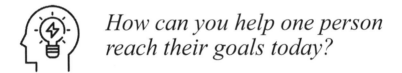 *How can you help one person reach their goals today?*

Sometimes CEOs get trapped by hiding behind the curtains of Compliance, Human Resources, Legal or the corner office. When this happens, we can become guarded with our answers, seeing our sentences before we speak them, and hiding behind closed doors, all of which cause others to perceive us as robotic corporate mouthpieces. That's not what a CEO is. A CEO is someone who works to serve others along with creating and executing the vision and mission of the organization.

There are No Bad CEOs

No leader purposely strives to be a bad CEO. They may fail, be moderately successful or come up short, but those results do not label them as bad. Poor results are from how they were raised, a lack of training, and their not taking advantage of opportunities to learn.

When a CEO starts losing, takes a beating, has a bad quarter, is criticized by the board of directors, hires the wrong people, or negotiates a bad acquisition, they react by starting to play the game safely. They may stop caring about the people they lead and focus on themselves and their reputation. Their decisions and behavior become based in fear, which leads to sub-par results. These CEOs are good people who yielded poor results, which lead to 'safe' or unproductive decisions. It doesn't make them bad it makes them human.

There are those with a weak character who only care about themselves and arrived at the top because of political favor or some type of nepotism. They may be causing the organization harm with selfishness or poor behaviors; however, I do not believe they set out to become ineffective leaders. They just didn't learn the skills of servant leadership.

How Anthony Became a CEO

Over the span of my career, I was sent to various parts of the USA for uncertain periods of time to serve others by improving results. Leadership asked me to move into these areas because they could trust me to take on the tough challenges with a positive can-do attitude. The new roles were always challenging because I was walking into underperforming operations with high expectations and tight timelines. Over the years, my skill set expanded and my reputation grew as a leader who achieved successful results, no matter the situation.

When I was asked to take on a challenging role in an uncomfortable new environment I simply said "Yes." If tomorrow I am asked to go somewhere else, I won't ask, "What is my title going to be?" The only question I will have is, "How can I help the organization, the clients, the community, and its people?"

I became a CEO and met the targets leadership gave me because I always brought my best to any challenge expected from me and my team. Over the years the challenges expanded and my leadership position kept rising higher to lead larger teams until I was asked to be the CEO of Marsh & McLennan Northeast. The latest request from leadership has moved me across the pond to lead a team as CEO of Marsh Commercial, in the U.K.

What it Takes to be Successful

To be successful you need to form good habits to improve your health, diet, sleep, and physical stamina. You must continue learning by reading different publications and books to help you see problems from a different point of view, which will open your mind to new ideas and creative possibilities.

It is easier to be stagnant, to remain unchanged, and do the bare minimum to get through life, however, your mission is to evolve to the best version of you. You have to be able to push yourself into uncomfortable situations, so you can grow, learn, and expand your sphere of influence. I challenge you to Push the Possible and achieve the greatness I know you are capable of reaching.

The servant-leader is servant first, it begins with a natural feeling that one wants to serve, to serve first, as opposed to, wanting power, influence, fame, or wealth.

- Robert K Greenleaf

You will need a blue-collar work ethic to get up every day, regardless of the environment. When I worked in construction, I did not have a choice. I had to go to work when it was cold, rainy, and hot. I had to go to work and climb the ladder to the roof, dig ditches and pound nails. I couldn't say, "I think I'll sleep in, or go home early because it might snow today." You can't afford to make that kind of call. If your goal is to be a leader, you have to show up and do your best work each and every day.

I once heard a Marine General say, "If you want to be successful you need to make your bed every morning." He was talking about more than making sure the blankets are neat before you leave for the day. He was talking about getting up and doing the job, even when no one else is watching.

19

Completing your daily tasks, no matter how insignificant, is about having the integrity to be honest with yourself and true to others, so you can look anyone in the eye with courage, knowing you can serve them to the best of your ability, every time because they matter.

Being a Leader is Hard

It is hard because sometimes we get our hearts broken. We think we did a good job, made the right commitment, applied the proper traits, and had the correct habits. Then somebody does not step up when we think they should. A decision is made which negatively affects us or does something to trigger the failure of our efforts. There will be times when people will not be there, even when they promised otherwise. During those moments you need to dig more deeply into yourself and deliver.

There will certainly be times when you will be disappointed and discouraged: it happens to all of us. How you react and move forward is what matters. Being diligent about having wins, experimenting, overachieving and surpassing goals will offset the troughs, so you can focus on the triumphs.

Leaders need to consistently show up and do what they have to do, regardless of the conditions or environment.

Welcome to the
Roots of Leadership Podcast with
Anthony C. Gruppo,
CEO, author, and motivator.

Anthony's mission is to help others weld their passion to their potential and increase their performance. Hear him go one-on-one with America's leaders and entrepreneurs. Each guest will share their innovations, concepts and ideas, which helped to make them and those they serve, successful.

Even the toughest shed a tear. They know raw emotion ignites a powerful internal motion.

Roots of Leadership
Gene Waddy

Diversant CEO and founder Gene Waddy has legacy on his mind as he leads Diversant, the largest African-American owned IT staffing and solutions firm in the US. From the inspiration of his father, to the motivation of his wife and children, Gene continues to strive for excellence.

He measures success by his impact on those around him, his contribution to the community, and the opportunities Diversant creates for others. His powerful story about a moment which seems like a setback to most, was truly the jumping off point for him to create his destiny.

The Interview

A: *This is Anthony Gruppo, welcome to today's episode of the Roots of Leadership Podcast. Gene Waddy is a visionary entrepreneur, the owner and CEO of Diversant, the nation's largest African American owned IT staffing and solutions firm. Welcome to the Roots of Leadership Podcast Gene.*

G: Thank you Anthony for having me on your show today.

I can't help but smile when I start to think about what Diversant is and when people tie it back to me, it makes me feel even better. I like it when people say, "Gene, Diversant is a reflection of you and your vision," but it's really about our hundred and fifty employees. Diversant does have some of my vision and ethics around diversity, inclusion, and community activism, but it really boils down to the delivery and excellence in everything we do. Our clients don't contract us because we're a diverse firm, they contract with us because we are one of the best in the business. I think this summarizes who we are and whom we aspire to be.

We're not done, we have some more hills to climb.

A: *No doubt, you will be successful Gene. We both come from blue-collar families. Tell us a little bit about when, as a youth, you started to understand what excellence was in a blue-collar environment.*

G: Thinking back on those years, I cannot help but smile. I think of helplessness. At the time, I worked for a very large staffing company when there were some changes at the top and the new team decided to go in a different direction. It was not a reflection on my performance. It was just a business decision and certain employees did not fit with the new go-forward plan. It was just business, but that didn't matter to little ol' me, who at that point, was solidly middle management. I thought I had to the world by the tail and I'd be there for another ten years.

When word came down about being laid off, the first thing I felt was shock. Then I remember saying to myself, "What am I going to tell my wife?" Kim is my high school sweetheart. I met her at William L. Dickinson High School, not far from where we're sitting right now in Teaneck, New Jersey. It is not a long commute home, and on the way to catch the train, I kept thinking, "What am I going to tell her?" I'm from Neptune, NJ which is not far from the ocean and in certain reflection points of my life I'm always pulled back to the ocean for some reason; like it's a place of calm and peace. Then a strange thing happened. I took the Jersey Coast train to Asbury Park instead of taking my normal train home. It was February and I was out on that jetty for a good thirty to forty minutes, just to breathe in the air and get my head and my emotions together. Then you know what happened? I started to feel a sense of freedom and empowerment, because at that point, I knew I had a chance to do something different, to chart a path for me and not one dictated by anybody else.

I got myself together, went home and told Kim. At this point I was an hour and a half late, so she is looking at me like, "What's going on?" I told her. Now to set the background, she was pregnant and we were closing on a house.

A: *A couple of extra stressors.*

G: Yeah just a couple, but you know, I told her, "Listen, honey, I got laid off." She looked at me for a minute and then I said, "Please don't worry," because I could tell she was getting a little shaky on me and I said to her, "Don't worry I might have a plan." She said, "What's your plan?" "I'm going to start my own IT staffing company." She started crying and I don't think she stopped until Sunday night because she thought I'd lost my mind.

After I got over the initial shock of what happened, I understood we bend but we don't break.

A: *There was something else you said, "There is never a right time to start a business." It is so true because every time I've taken a risk, if I had listened to the "Pundits" predicting the timing wasn't right, I would have missed a couple of opportunities. Gene, how did you know it was the time to take the leap because it was a bold move? You had a new baby on the way and you had a new house to pay for. What inside you said, I can do this right now?*

G: Anthony, that's a great question. I knew I had paid my dues. I had enough competency in the industry to make it a credible step. I'd been in the staffing business for twenty-five to twenty-six years. The timing was right for me because I wanted some control in my life. I felt adrift and even though it was for a short time, it was terrifying.

My dad taught us about working in a consistent job. He worked in the same company for thirty years. Thirty years! Most of the folks in our neighborhood were postmen, policemen, and folks who worked in factories. Those were jobs, maybe not for life, but it could easily be for twenty years or more. I decided the only way to get the security back, was to take it for myself, to control my destiny. I know it sounds new wave, getting in touch with yourself, but it was a basic blocking and tackling move. I already knew what I was doing. I was competent. I had relationships in the industry. I had references from very large Fortune 500 companies, who would become my clients once Diversant launched.

A: *While you were employed in the IT staffing business, you were doing the best you could to learn your core competency. Whatever you are doing, be amazing at it to prepare for those unplanned moments. The people who get surprised are the ones who were not preparing for it to happen, they swim to every shiny object, frequently switching jobs, and they wonder why they are never satisfied in their life, in their career.*

G: Well said, I couldn't have said it better. I have a saying, "The parachute will not open if you don't jump." Some of us jump willingly and some of us get pushed out of the plane. I got pushed. Sometimes the plane is on fire and you've got to make a decision, you've gotta jump since the parachute is not going to open unless you jump.

I'm always cautious when I do these kind of talks to not sound too cavalier about it because it is not an easy decision to make.

Being a CEO is not for everybody.

I look at it this way. If you take a look at my team, there's only one me, but there are a whole bunch of talented people around me. I would say a good portion of those folks are more talented than I am. I'm very happy and thankful for them because they make the business go forward. You cannot have a team full of A-personality alpha types, it's not going to work. I learned this early. I also learned to stay humble throughout this process, to deflect the praise and catch somebody doing a good job to give them praise.

A: *As a leader, you have to catch somebody doing well because too often we only talk to them when there is a problem. Gene, in your first year, on your own, you made three hundred thousand dollars in total revenue. I want to give the listeners a spectrum, if you don't mind, about how much your business has grown.*

G: Today, if everybody showed up to work, we are tracking about a hundred and seventy million a year. We have thirteen offices and have some great Fortune clients, plus we just rolled out a payroll solutions business about a year and a half ago and it has closed a nice chunk of business for us.

A: *Through-out all your success, you have stayed focused on the community with minority youth and you are also a member of Alpha Phi Alpha, the first African American fraternity in the nation. Whether it was lessons learned from a fraternity or being the son of parents from Harlem, let me ask you this Gene, how do you benefit from community?*

G: That's an easy one, because when the community prospers, we all prosper. It's about giving back, staying relevant, and there is some very shrewd business acumen at play.

Anthony, I'm shameless about talent, I'm always trying to spot the diamond in the rough, the next leader we may bring on board at Diversant as a salesperson, recruiter, or business leader. If the individual goes out and starts a business themselves, they definitely help the community. Some firms, which started due to my mentorship and coaching, have gone on to do great things. They will call me and say, "Gene, listen, we started, we're off and running and we just got an opportunity at X client, but they told us we need to have another firm come in to help us. It just so happens, Gene, you're on the supplier list at X company. How about doing a joint venture or let us come in as a second-tier supplier?" They may have better relationships than some of mine.

You have to develop a farm team, whether it's in business or your own HR strategy, you have to be bringing in talent, training them up, developing them, and then turning them loose. This is the key to sustaining growth and trusting them.

A: *You're touching on a key issue Gene. You and I, as CEOs, learned it never ends up the way we thought it would. We saw the initial vision of how we wanted it to go and when we got there, we discovered it was not even close. We work at it. We are happy it came together, but it is not what we initially envisioned. When people read your background, listen to the podcast today, they are going to say, this is a fearless guy. He's not afraid. Is there anything Gene Waddy is fearful of?*

G: Oh, yes, plenty of things. I'm amazed I got out of bed this morning and came on the parkway. Fearlessness is a bit of a misnomer. It is about managing the fear. If you're not afraid of something, there is probably something wrong with you, some wiring misalignment. It's about how you use fear. It can be destructive or constructive. I had to be taught this. I didn't get to watch people around me demonstrate how to use fear. I had to be taught how to use my emotions to move forward.

My biggest fear is gaining all the material trappings of wealth and then losing my family, losing my soul, and losing my connection to the community. Now that I've had a certain degree of success, I am surrounded by people who have it completely backward. They have the three houses, the boat, the plane, they're on their fifth wife, the kids can't stand them, they have health problems, and all sorts of things are falling apart. I don't want that. When I go home to the Glory, because we don't live forever, I want people to say, "You know Gene Waddy, right? He was a good guy. He helped me put my kids through school and he was always there to help." Then I'll know I've done it right.

A: *Legacy is not in material possessions. It is in the material we all posses to make each other better. If I cannot put myself in the moments where fear is present, then I need to be afraid because I will not be challenging myself. I think I've become more of a product than a person because I'm a product of all the people who made me realize how much I have to learn every day.*

G: Anthony, I'm writing this down.

A: *Gene, let's change gears and talk about the people we have around us. When you're doing an interview, talking to a new colleague or potential client, what is the most important thing? Listeners will often ask me, "How do I improve my interview skills? How do I show a more of an impressive side of myself?" What gets you to pay attention to a person's fabric when you first meet them?*

31

G: That's a great question. I look for a story, a narrative, not what it says on the piece of paper, that is irrelevant. The way I look at the resume is, you made it this far, you must have half a clue about what you're doing, but that is not what I hire on. It is about connectivity, something authentic, something that reaches out and touches me. One of my favorite questions to ask is, what did your Mom do? What did your Dad do? When you were growing up what sports did you play? Talk to me about when something didn't go right in life. I want to know how they handle adversity because I don't need fair weather employees. I need people who can manage when the seas are calm and when the seas are rocky. I believe we're in it together.

Where are your roots? We are set from the time we are small children. As adults, we are only bigger with better toys, hopefully, but who we are is set early on. So, I want to know, were you an only child? Did you have a large family? If Mom and Dad were both neurosurgeons, and you are fresh out of college showing up to the interview with an overly expensive handbag you may not need this job, or you may not be willing to row with the rest of the team or make the necessary sacrifices.

A: *There are people from all types of backgrounds, who display all kinds of courage and initiative, but you're right, as far as the story is concerned. For the listeners who hear Gene and me talking today, think about asking these questions of an employer. You can turn the table and not answer those standard interview questions.*

I like to ask the people, "Why will your colleagues at the Marsh & McLennan Agency Northeast be better because they met you?" I want to hear the answer. I want to know what it will look like when you are frustrated. What will happen to the organization because you are frustrated? Gene, can you control your emotions? Can you stay calm, regardless of the storm raging around you? You have dealt with a few storms. How do you prepare for those large decisions?

G: I was the type of kid who went off into a corner to figure things out on my own. As I got older, particularly in college, I learned to solve really large problems. You have to have a team around you to get different viewpoints, weigh them, and be an active listener, which is something I had to be taught. When I'm faced with large decisions, either in my personal or professional life, the first thing I try to do is to be quiet because I can't think when there is a bunch of craziness, a hurricane, or people emotionally losing their heads around me. The second thing I do, which I learned over thirty years ago, is to consult people who know what they're talking about and it's a different group of people, depending on what the problem is. If I had to turn back the clock to my high school and college years, one of the things I would have done earlier is build a network of those types of people. I have a business board and I have a life board of people around me.

When I'm mentoring young folks both professionally and personally because you can have a person who's got the best pedigree in the world, but if their personal life is a disaster, you're never going to get a hundred percent.

A: *Let's stay with a concept you the listeners heard us talking about - building a Personal Board of Directors. Let's expand on what you're saying because you are giving incredible advice.*

33

Today, there are five generations in the workforce. We have people who were born in the forties and fifties through to the early two thousands. I dislike labeling. I am not a fan of the term millennial because there have been energetic, lazy, aggressive, and calm people in every generation. It is nothing new for young people to come into the workforce and struggle with their 'new' reality.

One message I want to make clear to everyone, not just the young adults, but to all generations in the workforce, as leaders, it is not our job to make you happy. It is our job to make you better. Happiness is your issue.

A Personal Board of Directors will help you to navigate the waters toward your Possible. They will help you to define what happiness is for you and how to go out and grab it. When you create a Personal Board of Directors, surround yourself with people who will ask the tough questions, the type of people who will force you to dig for the truth and find the right answers. If you take nothing else from today's podcast, I would encourage you to build a Personal Board.

Gene, I know you're a planner. What is next in the strategic plan of Gene Waddy, which would have me pause, go get a sandwich, and some energy because it's about to get crazy. What is it?

G: We rolled out into the payroll business and it's off to a flying start. I think this section of our business, in the next three years, could be a hundred-million-dollar business on its own. However, what I really want to do, and this is going sound kind of strange, but my passion is mentorship, developing others, coaching others, helping others. I would like to open an academy where we could develop our youth, particularly African American males.

I get pulled in so many different directions with business and my life. I have two kids, a wife, and three dogs. I'm a busy guy, but I always feel as though my calling is pulling me toward something and I think that something is an academy where I can pour what I have into some deserving children who will become better people. Maybe there is something missing in their life and I can help fill a gap. It's something which has been bugging me for the last ten to fifteen years.

Having a business is like a wrestling match, it's never really over, it's changing and reinventing itself, but at fifty, you start to see the world differently. You start thinking about legacy, about the exit strategies. You start to think about those things. What will you do afterward to sustain yourself and make yourself happy? You start to think about those things because the businesses are only vehicles to do great things. Money is fine. You have to have money to do a lot of things in the world. I get it, but it's about people. The people who work for us are part of the family, we want to see them prosper, see their kids prosper. The business now, I'm proud to say, would go on without me. That means a lot.

A: *A true sign of great leadership is when we can build something around a model, not around a man or a woman. When you said, you start to think about legacy, Gene, I would encourage you to start to think about defining your legacy now, not later. What do you want it to look like when it's over? Define over, what does it look like for you? Is it a re-engineering versus a retirement?*

35

Gene, there were times during this discussion where I forgot we were putting this out to thousands of people. It felt like it was two men in a room who are in some ways still trying to figure it out every day.

I want to recap for a moment what Gene mentioned in five areas. If you listen to what he said, he takes his vision, his passion, and he connects it to a calling. He stayed in his core competency, as he built his business and his life. He looks for the advantage, every opportunity, and he has a fearless love of risk. Gene lives to mentor in an environment where everyone sells and he keeps his core, his ethics, his metal of being a man. It is impressive.

G: Well, I appreciate that. It's very humbling to hear you say it. Talking about 'everyone sells,' I struggled with this early on. I'm an engineer, I have an engineering degree, so, the biggest struggle for me was to really understand, everyone sells. I didn't understand

To maximize your potential, do not make excuses, do not blame, but constantly reach for the next rung on the ladder that challenges you to be uncomfortable.

what sales was. I always thought sales was like the used car guy, or retail product, but it's not. It about being an advocate for the client. Those guys who are the best at it are the most genuine. The people who speak from the heart and are trying to show the person the right way and why, they invite everybody to feel like they have something out of the deal. Once it sunk in, I was off to the races.

A: *The greatest salesperson is concerned about their client's mission, not their commission, and they live with a passion to serve. Servant leaders chase solutions.*

Gene, thank you for being on my show today. It's been an amazing honor.

G: Thank you for having me.

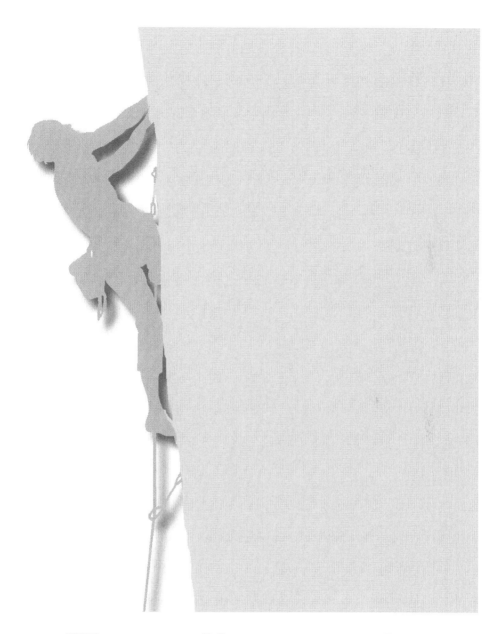

Excellence in Change

Sometimes after your best effort you may feel as though you are alone in the challenge.

Find comfort in knowing your effort is the catalyst for someone's dream to come true.

You are never alone.

When life throws curve balls, will you strike out or hit it out of the park? Having a life, business and a career plan are all very important to achieving success. However, don't be married to them or set them in stone, because life sometimes has its own plan for you.

Unexpected events can derail the best laid plans and end the journey we are on. Disappointment can either cause you to throw in the towel or put you on a path you never imagined possible. Keeping your eyes on future possibilities instead of past losses will help to manage the negative emotions which come along with disappointment.

Whether you can weather the storm of unexpected change depends on how you manage your thoughts, your emotions, and your attitude. You are the captain of your ship, so take responsibility for those choices you have control over to discover the enhanced opportunities around you.

What Gene Waddy Taught Us

To excel you must possess a relentless drive, show up, and be prepared. There is no guarantee you will keep the job you have today and when something happens you must process your emotional state, so you can more clearly see your options, make new decisions, and work hard to make your new path a success.

The best type of business to start is within the industry you have experience and connections. The best time to start a business is when you take the leap of faith out of the plane and do it because there is no 'right time.' Taking control of your future by starting a company can be scary for those who are close to you because their lives are going to be affected too.

To build a successful business you need to surround yourself with talented, hard working, and smart people who bring different skills to the table. The key is to find potential leaders, train them, bring them up and then let them fly. Giving back, mentoring, and helping others will lead to more opportunities and a more fulfilled life. No one can do it all on their own. You need to find a support network, mentors, and people whom you trust to sit on a Personal Board of Directors to help you, regardless of whether you are a CEO, a salesperson, a manager, or a receptionist. Success is about people.

Fear is a reality but what you do with it will define the outcomes.

I was blessed to have the support of a loving family.

Find Your Success

Define your career and where you want to be by visualizing your future. Let your imagination go to places you are scared to go and see what is possible. Envision where you want to be, find out how to get there by learning new things, talking to people, and meeting visionaries who will help you dream an even bigger dream. As you discover how to get where you want to be, you will need to write a plan outlining the steps you will take.

To grow within an organization, you must never think about your job as a position in a company. It's a launching pad. Reach out to people who are five levels above you and ask if they will sit down with you. Interview them by asking what their day-to-day is like. Ask them about their vision, how they got started, and get to know them. Leaders love to share their stories and advice; however, few people reach out. Most people sit at their desks hoping someone will notice them, too afraid to reach out to the leaders in their company and are left wondering why they never get anywhere.

After I gave a speech at New York University, an emerging leader asked me questions about Marsh & McLennan. She spoke multiple languages, and was an avid reader who was working on a Master's degree. We hied her as an intern at the Marsh & McLennan Northeast Agency because she stepped up. She didn't wait for a standing invitation. She saw where she wanted to go in her career, wanted to learn more about the industry, and took action.

> *I was blessed to work with amazing colleagues.*

When Opportunities Happen

When I was in my early twenties, I was working in the construction industry. I knew I could do more, but I grew up in a blue-collar environment, so I thought, if a labor job was okay for my parents, it'll be okay for me.

Then one day, I was on the job, building the Berkheimer building in Pennsylvania when I started talking to members of the Berkheimer family who were on-site overseeing construction. At one point they said, "You know, you don't strike us as someone who is going to be in construction all his life." I told them why I didn't envision a career as a laborer either. Next thing you know, because I was local, they introduced me to a leader of one of the local banks. Each person they introduced me to said, "This guy's not just a construction worker." However, I was a construction worker. I wore work boots, a hard hat, gloves, jeans and a T-shirt. I had no badge, no title, not even a corporate business card. Yet, I spoke with energy, passion, drive, and focus, which is what set me apart from others.

The next thing I knew, I was being asked if I wanted to learn the banking business or the insurance, real estate, or finance industries. I chose finance and became a bill collector, which was the launching pad to the adventure of a lifetime. We might ask ourselves, was it luck?

I don't think so. I engaged with business owners when no one else I worked with on the construction crew did. They believed it wasn't their place to speak to the owners. I was the only one who took the time to talk to the guys in suits. No one else was willing to step outside of their comfort zone and make the leap into a different life.

I think it was positioning. I think it was energy. I think it was courage and drive. I was willing to put myself into uncomfortable situations. It wasn't natural for me to walk up to business leaders and ask them questions, as I was not sure if it was the proper thing to do, but I wanted to know what it took to wear a business suit and to be the one making the decisions. I wanted to Push the Possible in my life and see how far I could go.

When I was trying to learn multi-disciplines in business insurance, other people in the office tried to keep me in a box by being unhelpful and blocking my efforts to grow. I knew I had to teach myself things about finance, business insurance, operations, employee health and benefits, retirement services, and personal lines of insurance. I expected it was going to be tough because I was new to those disciplines in the industry. When I asked questions, people tried to block me by telling me, "You don't need to know, just be good at what you do and stay over on your side of the fence."

It was not easy to find the information at that time because the internet was not what it is today. I had to rely on others to help me find the sources of information I needed, and most people were not willing to help. I did not let it stop me, I pushed on by learning as much as I could about the various disciplines in the insurance industry and after a while, the more senior insurance agents started to come to me for answers.

This is when I discovered the reason people did not want to help was because they didn't know the answers, not because they did not want me to succeed. This realization helped me to gain confidence. I wanted to be valuable to those with whom I worked; constantly learning, growing, and pushing up.

45

If you want to be valuable to the company you work for, be valuable to yourself. Put on the correct uniform, be it a suit or work boots and a hard hat. Leave your problems at home, focus on your tasks, and be helpful to your colleagues. Do not see them as just people sitting in a cubicle next to you. Do not see them as competition. When you help them, they will help you because they will start talking about you and then opportunities will appear. This is how you will advance from one position to the next, through good work, goodwill, good humor, and a caring attitude. Leaders and managers are looking to advance and team up with the people who have the skills and talents they may not have.

My podcast producer, Caryn Ojeda, is always positive and always has a good attitude. She never has a bad day, ever. There are days I would complain to her, but she has never complained to me. I see in her what I want in myself. I'm searching for people who can apply a band-aid to my cut when I'm hurt. They can patch me up and put me back in the game. I do the same for them.

At Marsh & McLennan Northeast, they have a community, not a culture. Cultures are simple. Everybody wants to work in a good culture. It is not hard to do, if we are just decent to each other. When you build a team of people who support each other, help one another, and push each other to be better, you are forming a rich community. Leaders want people who are energetic, focused, have a can-do attitude, and don't take credit for work. They never say, "Look at what I did." They always say, "Look at what somebody else did." They always congratulate others for their success.

This is the type of person leaders want on their team.

When Things Go Wrong

Too often people will say well, "It's business, it is not personal," to make themselves feel good when they fail, but they are not doing themselves any favors. When you do not get a deal, it is personal. You've lost revenue and you may not have the money you need to support your family. If you did not get a job or something bad happens, it is personal.

When leaders say, "It's not personal, it's just business," we are trying to put a salve over the cut we just created. We are trying to stitch you up, put a bandage on it and send you on your way so we don't feel bad, but it is also personal. If an employee personally did not give it everything they had and leadership had to make the decision to let them go, it will affect the employee on a personal level. Leadership does not want people to fail. No one wants to let someone go. Leaders want people to succeed and stay on with the company.

When people get down on themselves, they are slow in producing, stop growing, and they lose value to the team. The thing is, these people were very good once. What happened from the time they were hired and were stellar, to their failing and having to be let go?

If something does not go your way, it is not the be-all and end-all. Make what happened personal, but do not let it paralyze you. People who get paralyzed by victim mentality start thinking, "I'm not going to try again because it is too painful." Remember you are good enough to be successful. Life will not beat you down, you will overcome adversity. Understand the personal ramifications of your setbacks, learn from your mistakes, find out how you could have done it better, and try again.

As a leader, you may be buying the "It's just business" lie and you start to see people as commodities, as numbers, not as people. You may become more concerned about how people can help your mission, vision, enterprise, and not how you can help them grow and succeed. If you begin to make 'business only' decisions by asking questions like, "Who is less expensive to promote? Who will accept a smaller bonus?," the people on your team will stop trying and will become a barrier to your bottom line instead of improving upon it.

Sometimes, leaders have to let people go for a several reasons and some of them have nothing to do with the person's performance and everything to do with business. Sales may be down, the company is pivoting or new management has come in and wants to make an impression. Whatever the reason, the result is the same. You are out of a job and looking at an uncertain future.

You have a choice when this happens, you can take on the challenge of discovering a new dream or you can wallow in self-pity and go nowhere.

The Place of Fear

Fear is a strong emotion meant to keep us safe from the real dangers to our well-being, health, and lives. In today's world, we fear unreal dangers, which are introduced to us through news, Hollywood, marketing, and our political leaders. The more we have, the more we fear losing it and then we spend more energy protecting what we have than risking to get more.

Anxiety is on the rise in teens and young adults, as they strive to do everything they need to do in a day. It is becoming an epidemic in our society as people live in fear of losing, being judged, and failing. Many give up or don't even try because fear tells them they won't make it, so they might as well escape into movies, video games, social media, alcohol, drugs, or a host of other addictive escapist behaviors.

Some people wake up afraid of what will happen next, when the shoe will drop, which curve ball will hit them, or when the rug will be pulled. The more these people fear, the more their fears are proven right as they lose again and again. If you are in a place of fear, you've already lost. If you dwell or ruminate in a place of fear, you are in a losing position. To overcome your fears and move forward, acknowledge it, understand what you are afraid of, and then decide if the fear is real or manufactured.

How much money do you have in the bank? How much do you need to make rent? What will it take to get it? Can you get a job? If you cannot find work, can you find a project or a contract? Have you looked hard enough? Be honest with yourself. Have you truly done everything you possibly can to find work to pay the bills? You may not like the solution, but you have to realize it is only a short-term situation and you can handle the situation by making the necessary choices to move forward.

I have found people I can trust throughout my life and have surrounded myself with helpful people by being helpful myself. I start by helping others first and learning about them as I do, this way I find the people I can trust to help me when I have confidence cracks.

I've been afraid. I know what it feels like to be disappointed. I've been anxious. I have believed I wasn't enough and didn't have what it took. I know the taste of fear. I just don't swallow it. I roll the fear around in my mouth, use my other senses to touch it, smell it, experience it, to get to know the edges of it. I know what I don't want to happen. I know what I do want to happen. I understand what I am really afraid of, and then, I drive myself past it.

Confidence Cracks

Where do CEOs of major companies go when they're struggling with confidence issues and questions? They certainly can't call the Chairman of the Board and say, "I just don't know what I'm doing right now. I'm having a confidence crack." Probably not the best career move. It is not a good idea for them to walk amongst their colleagues with their head down, shoulders drooped and announce to everyone in the building, "I'm having a confidence crack. I don't know what to do today."

Everyone needs help. Even the leaders of international corporations need people whom they can trust to bounce ideas off of, discuss confidence cracks with, and help them to create their plans. The people they go to for help make up their Personal Board of Directors.

If you want to become a leader, only you can make it happen.

Personal Board of Directors

When I wrote my first book, *Creating Reality, a Guide to Personal Accomplishment*, I designed a technique to help leaders when they have a confidence crack. It is often recommended that you surround yourself with quality people who will challenge you. I do not think this approach is good enough. No matter your title or place in life, you need a Personal Board of Directors if you are serious about becoming a leader and seeing yourself as a CEO. Your Personal Board of Directors will listen to your business and life plans, ask hard questions, give real feedback, and hold you accountable. I have been blessed to have great people on my board over the years. One of the best was Monique ter Haar, who co-authored my book, *Six Degrees of Impact*.

We wrote the book to incorporate business modeling with personal integration or models. I asked Monique to join me because she is a Behavioral Health Specialist. Together we studied why people do the things they do when they are under pressure, to develop a new organization development method, which I've used at every company I've led to success. When you find someone like her on your board, you can understand the important things and how you make decisions.

Your Personal Board of Directors

Whom you choose to sit on your Personal Board of Directors is vital to your success, so choose wisely. Imagine you are the CEO and have total ownership of your company. Who would you recruit to discuss your life and your business plan? Well, you might recruit family members to be your support people and the managers inside the company.

The great problem solvers listen, think about solutions and facilitate the discussion because it isn't about them. It is about you and they are only there to help you. You need to choose people whom you trust because you will share your life and business plan with these individuals. They should also trust your ability to run the company and believe you are capable of success. If they do not believe in you, their ability to help you will be limited by their own false assumptions. Your board must be willing to listen to you, ask questions, and provide feedback to help you make better decisions.

Where do These People Come From?

Often people tell me, "I don't know the people you know, so I don't know who to recruit." You do, you only have to think about it. You can find them in your community, amongst your friends, and in your workspace. If you reach out into the community, people will help you.

I reached out to people whom I didn't know and I said, "I've read your book, I follow your social media and I like your values. My name is Anthony Gruppo and I have a Personal Board of Directors. Would you consider being interviewed for a spot?" No one has ever said no. I limit their commitment to a one or two year term position because as we grow, we need different people to challenge us, help us see things from a fresh perspective and discover new opportunities.

Personal Board members can come from all walks of life. Look for a diversity of thought leaders who can challenge you. Find people who have experience in various industries and can give you a different point of view. You are looking for: A consultant. A strategist. A facilitator. A closer.

Think about it this way, great leaders are consultative, they are strategists, they are facilitators, and they are closers. You will need all four types of people on your Personal Board of Directors.

You can Find People Anywhere

The first person you need to find is someone who believes in you and will tell you why you are going to succeed. Then trust and clarify what they say. Have an honest debate with them. Remember the people whom you put on your board are there to tell it to you straight and they won't lie to make you feel better.

Chose successful, smart, and confident people who want to help you realize your potential. Be mindful to surround yourself with people who are not too emotionally invested in your financial situation.

Embrace your positive emotions, energy, passion and drive. These emotions will pave the way to success.

Types of Board Members

Consultants are people you go to with questions to get advice, solutions, and answers. They are considered experts in their field and industry. They are the experienced leaders.

Strategists are people whom you go to for help coming up with ideas. They have a natural talent for seeing the big picture and how things fit together. These are the visionary leaders who are innovative and creative in their problem solving.

Facilitators are the people you consult when you are stumped and need to find others who can help you. They know everyone and have a great reputation for finding resources. They are well connected networkers who build amazing relationships.

Closers are people whom you go to when things need to get done. They are talented professionals with the gift of matching solutions to needs and moving a project to closure. They know what needs to be done and know how to get it done.

Push Your Possible

Excellence in Change

This is the part of the book where you dive deeply into the concepts to form your own opinions, make plans, and set goals.

I encourage you to mark up the pages and make this book a resource for your life journey.

Want to share your thoughts with me on social media? Tag me in your Twitter or LinkedIn post and use the hashtag, #PushersofPossible.

Winning Attitude

See yourself winning and start making small incremental moves and you will get there. What do you have to do today to move toward a winning attitude?

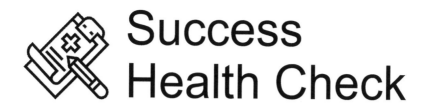# Success
Health Check

If you lost your job tomorrow what would you do?

_____

_____

_____

Would you want to start your own business as Gene Waddy did or seek a new position with another company?

_____ Look for a new position

_____ Start my own company

Are you prepared if you lose your job? _____ Yes _____ No

Do you have 6 months of expenses in the bank? _____ Yes _____ No

Have you been actively networking with people who may be able to help you find an opportunity? _____ Yes _____ No

Is your LinkedIn up to date? _____ Yes _____ No

Do you have a portfolio of your work? _____ Yes _____ No

Are you building a personal brand online? _____ Yes _____ No

Challenge

Create a Plan B, just in case the unthinkable happens.

A Personal Board

Get started on building your board of directors. Make a list of the ten people you spend the most time with. These are the people who are a fixture in your life. Start at #10 and countdown to #1.

10.

9.

8.

7.

6.

5.

4.

3.

2.

1.

Your Dream Team

Go wild with your imagination and create a top ten Personal Board of Directors dream team. It can be anyone, you don't have to know them, choose anyone, dream big!! Start from #10 and countdown to #1

10.

9.

8.

7.

6.

5.

4.

3.

2.

1.

Your Need

Think about the advice you need. What issues in your professional and personal lives do you want support with? Riff below, no order of preference or intensity.

Assess the Possibilities

Go back to the list of people you know. Take a moment to assess the list to determine which of the ten can you trust to give you good advice?

Go back to your dream team list and think about the qualities each of them would bring to your Personal Board of Directors. Why do you want them on your team? Whom do you know or have access to who possesses those same qualities?

Go back to your needs list. Write down the name of someone from your lists whom you believe can help you with each item. Why do you think they are the best choice?

Your Personal Board

Make a final list of those people you are going to approach, why them, and how best to contact them.

10.

9.

8.

7.

6.

5.

4.

3.

2.

1.

Assess Your Team

Now that you have an idea about whom you can trust to give you good advice and which members of the dream team have the qualities you need to succeed, sort the names to see what a well-rounded Personal Board will look like for you.

Who are the Consultants?

Who are the Strategists?

Who are the Facilitators?

Who are the Closers?

Guidelines

You need a clear idea of how you want your Personal Board to operate. Will they meet with you on a regular basis? Will you have phone conversations or face to face meetings? Is it formal? Casual? Do you want to give each position a limited timeframe or an indefinite position? This is your Personal Board; how will it operate?

How to Ask

For some, the hardest part is asking someone to be a mentor, an advisor, or a member of their Personal Board. Write down the points you want to communicate when asking someone and then... ASK.

Name:

What makes this person a good choice?

What do you want them to advise you about?

What value and skills do they bring to the table?

Have insatiable courage in yourself. A belief so strong in your ability, that no one, I mean no one, can deter you from your ultimate desire to succeed.

Roots of Leadership
Jennifer Walsh

Jennifer Walsh writes, advises on beauty and wellness, appears on television, and started her first business before she turned thirty.

Throughout her life, she experienced daunting setbacks, which could have resulted in giving up, however, by embracing change, keeping a grateful outlook, and a positive attitude, she picked up many important life lessons while building a successful brand.

She brought her love of nature together with passion for health by interviewing guests about what makes a leader productive while walking in New York's Central Park. She is a leader who is the definition of a positive powerhouse of the Possible.

The Interview

A: *Hi, this is Anthony Gruppo, and welcome to today's episode of the Roots of Leadership. I have been waiting to interview Jennifer Walsh for a long time. I am so excited to have her on the show today. Welcome to the Roots of Leadership.*

J: Thank you Anthony, I'm very excited to be here.

A: *Jennifer, I want to take a moment to let the listeners know about some of your background because it is impressive. You are an entrepreneur, a stellar athlete, a writer with two manuscripts, a long time TV celebrity of twenty years, a beauty expert, and my favorite, the host of the Walk with Walsh Program, which you do in Central Park. It's a truly an innovative interview style. Congratulations.*

J: I'm honestly thrilled. I've been waiting so long to come and do this with you and am honored. I'm motivated and inspired by you and your work ethic. I'm thrilled to be sitting here with you today.

A: *Thank you, Jennifer. You are such a servant leader because you always exude humility. Let's jump right in. What advice do you have for women who lead people or are starting a business?*

J: I didn't really plan on the heading up Beauty Bar or to build what it became. I wanted to do something I loved to provide for myself and liked to do every day. I was turning my passion into a job for me. When it grew and grew and grew, I wasn't expecting it. I didn't know how to do it and had to figure it out as I went along. I was twenty-eight years old and I didn't know much about retail, how to create purchase orders, how to run a store, or anything to do with growing a company. I had to surround myself with good people and ask lots of questions.

A: *Twenty-eight years old, where did the courage come from?*

J: I don't know. I think I felt it in my gut Anthony. I thought if I don't do this, someone else will. It was one of those things where everyone told me I shouldn't do it. I was working at Merrill Lynch and was also a makeup artist at the time. I was Merrill Lynch by day, a makeup artist at night. I know, it was a really weird combination. I love makeup artistry and was learning how to do it. Then I started doing makeup for Jessica Simpson, Justin Timberlake, John Travolta, and other celebrities. I had this idea to take beauty out of a department store setting into a boutique with a non-sales approach to buying beauty products in a warm and inviting retail environment.

My parents said, "Don't do it." My friends said, "Don't do it." Everyone I went to said, it's the dumbest idea they'd heard because no one will ever leave a department store to go shop for makeup. I took $30,000 in savings and did it anyway. In the end, I revolutionized the industry.

A: *I want to reflect on this idea for a moment. It is not just the courageousness of taking on something, it was welded to your competitive nature. Here is Jennifer Walsh, entrepreneur, author, beauty expert, athlete and TV celebrity. It seems as though you do many distinct things, when really, you are a competitive woman who is courageous and going to achieve what she wants. Is that accurate?*

J: Wow, I've never heard it said in that manner. It's a really good point. I am very competitive. When I feel something in my bones

72

I want to go after it because I feel like if I can do it, then I want to make a difference. I want to pay it forward by adding value to people.

I realized after I started Beauty Bar, it wasn't about selling products, it was about storytelling. I realized, I could be an active part of a community, no matter how big or how small and make people feel comfortable in my environment by making them feel as though they're in my home. It's the best feeling in the world. I had five-year olds to eighty-year olds coming in, and everyone is treated the same way. It's a matter of setting a precedence for people knowing I would treat them with integrity and respect. It was a great feeling.

A: *Yes, I think as I listen to you, something for the listeners maybe to think about is, we all have the moment when we feel courageous, but when the obstacles and barriers hit us, that is when we need to have our competitiveness kick in and carry us forward. When you faced obstacles, what was your mindset?*

J: That's a really good point because I've had a lot of obstacles. I had to sell Beauty Bar after the 2008 market crash. I discovered my bills were not being paid by my CFO and there was an unveiling of things which were utterly shocking to me. It was very hard for me to see what was happening in my business. Then Quincy, who owns diapers.com and soap.com, called me with an offer to buy Beauty Bar because they wanted to add a high-end beauty product to their business model. Then Amazon bought Quincy. It was an interesting time and hard because I had employees and I had to close stores. I moved from Florida back to New York to work with the new Beauty Bar team. Plus, I was going through a divorce at the same time. It was major stress with a lot of life lessons. I think the most important part was I kept a level head about it all because if I had let all the

73

stresses show, it would have affected the people who counted on me. No one saw me off balance. I let myself say, "Okay, there is a reason for this, and I have to keep going." When people say, "Amazon ultimately owns Beauty Bar. How cool is that?" They don't understand the full story.

A: *There is something so powerful in your story Jennifer. Let's tap the brakes for a moment because when you said it is you, it is your heart, it is your mindset, it is all the things which make a strong leader, however, to others it is hidden. You have the ability to keep going with a positive mindset by taking the personal part out of the equation. Many of the listeners cannot do it. Everybody gets embroiled in what is happening to them personally. How did you manage to move beyond the personal?*

J: It was hard Anthony, really hard. Things can become very toxic and then your entire environment becomes toxic, or you can say, "Okay, I'm in this for the ride, for the experience". My whole life changed and I was no longer associated with the business I created. I was the Beauty Bar lady, the soap lady, I was a wife, I was a business owner, and all of a sudden, I was none of them. My identity was attached to business and I felt a loss of identity for a while. It was a tough year.

A: *It was a tough year?! You are a tough woman. I want to step back to something you said earlier about how you found your passion. Many great leaders say they found their passion and chased a dream. I often say to people, "Weld your passion to your potential and your performance will improve." A lot of people say to me, "I'm not passionate about anything." They have become sucked into routine to the point where passion evaporates. What would you say about passion?*

J: I think it's there. I think everyone gets in this zone of complacency, like they're in the shower, and already thinking about everything else they have to do in a day. They are everywhere else, instead of in the present moment. I've had lots of conversations around passion with my loved ones. We get sucked into a trap of focusing on where do we have to be next, instead of saying, "Wow, smell the beautiful aroma of the coffee, the flowers, and finding the passion in what we do and what drives us." I think we have to stop and recognize what's driving us every day, besides money, because it cannot be money at the end of the day. I know many of us are in jobs because of paychecks. I understand all of this and how, at the same time, we can't live without passion.

A: *At Marsh & McLennan Northeast, we constantly try to chase the mission of the client, not the commission. You have made a lot of large decisions in your life and some of them were thrust upon you. How do you prepare for large decisions?*

J: I don't know if you can prepare for them so much as understand who you are. It's taken me a long time to know who I am. In my 40s, I feel much more secure with who I am and saying, "Okay, I know this is going to hurt, but I have my health to stand on, I have my faith, and I have my family. I ultimately know, I will be okay. No matter what is shaken around me, I'm going to be okay." I think it is a matter of being in the right mindset, the right place in your life, to say, "I'm scared. I don't know what's to going happen next. Who should I turn to because I need help?" There have been times when I didn't know what to do, for instance, when the divorce happened, when I sold the company and when I started another company. There have been times in my life when I needed help. I would text SOS to my friends because I needed someone to talk to, I wanted to walk in the park with someone for fresh air, or I needed some new eyes on a problem. It is good to surround yourself with good people.

A: *As I watched your work on Walk with Walsh, I paid close attention to the behavioral patterns to get to know you. The program is a haven for you, isn't it? It is not a business.*

J: Yeah, absolutely. I didn't know it was a haven to be honest. I grew up going to Central Park. My grandparents had their very first date in Central Park, I didn't even know until after my grandpa passed. I spent every morning and evening in Central Park walking my dog and thought I was only going for my dog. Then my dog passed away and I kept going. I realized I was going longer and more often to the park. It was drawing me to it and I wanted to go there because it always made me feel good, even when I was going through my divorce. Some people turn to drugs, or alcohol, or whatever it might be, to feel better - the park is my tonic of choice.

A: *It became a creative haven for you. You even equated it to exercise and fitness because exercise is even more effective in a green environment. It is fascinating to me.*

J: I really love being outside. Two years ago, I started reading and studying what was happening. Then I started being with other people, neuroscientists, to find out what goes on with our brains when we are in nature.

A: *You have become the Pied Piper of leadership. Who were some of the greatest influences in your life?*

J: There have been a few. My parents; I think I'm so lucky to have the parents I have. They were given to me as a gift.

They've been so generous with their love, their time, and understanding of my journey, which is different from theirs. My dad was an FBI agent and my mom was a stay at home mother. She was so kind and loving and was always so supportive of all my endeavors. However, when I said, "I'm going to start my own company," they were both very concerned. My dad said, "You know, this is going to be very time consuming, it is going to take over, and don't you want a real job, with real money?" Then when I started the Beauty Bar, they understood what it meant to my soul, what it meant to the community, and they became really active in it. They have been my biggest influences, along with my twin sister. I think we choose the people we want around us and as we get older, we get to say, "That's bad energy and I don't have time for it." I want good people around me because the right people bring goodness to the table.

A: *I think you are right. Sometimes we devote our time to the wrong people. We end up giving too much and being a giver versus being a receiver. Do you think the greatest leaders and overachievers are a little bit selfish?*

J: Yeah, I've seen it and not in a bad way. A lot of people want to please people, especially when you're just starting out and you don't know what the path is going to look like. You want to do everything with everyone, and you want everyone to like you. I realized, after starting my first company, people aren't going like you, regardless of how nice you might be to them. You can't have everyone like you, there's just no way, do not even try.

A: *If you don't want a critic, then don't try anything new. Loved ones are worried when we start something new, however, as we succeed, it actually pulls them forward. There are people for whom* *you have been a role model. They saw Jennifer Walsh achieving and wanted to follow in your footsteps.*

I remember dropping out of college, being a construction worker, repossessing cars, and when I said I was going to write a book, people said, "Write a book? You shouldn't even write a sentence." Now after book two, three and four, they look at it differently. Do you feel like you inspired others to go for it?

J: I don't know, but I do know I always wanted to be there for other people. I never felt like it always had to be my rodeo.

I wanted other people to say, "Hey, I want to be in the same rodeo with you, I want to be a part of this, or how can we work together and collaborate?" Because I think we are much better together than separate. I try and tell the truth because sometimes people say, you are so lucky, you've done this, you've had that, you've been here, and you've been there. They don't know about all the work. They see me through rose colored glasses.

I like to be honest, to tell the truth whenever possible, because so many young women and young men whom I've talked to around the world, see the cover of Entrepreneur Magazine, or Forbes, and say, that is who I want to be like. Why do you want to be like them? What is it you are creating? Is it the fame you're going after? Or do you want to build a company you love because so many people right now are looking at Shark Tank and thinking I'm going to create a business so I can cash out in five years. It makes me want to cry because I don't think it's the right purpose. People see others and it looks so easy. They think it took two years or five years. Most of these people have been working ten, fifteen, maybe twenty years in their specific field.

A: *I looked at your Instagram and discovered that Jennifer Walsh started on Instagram in January 2011. What is the purpose, value, and objective for you with social media?*

J: I love it, because for me, it's always been about telling stories. I'm a social person by nature. I've always loved Twitter. I like using all the platforms. People whom I work with will only Snapchat or they're only on Instagram. If you have a story to tell, it has to be natural, it has to be on all platforms, however, you have to tell the story on each one differently. So many people are just trying to push a product or a sale. I think you have to give, like you do Anthony. You are always giving information and valuable lessons. Whenever I see your tweet, I think, I needed this today. I need a voice in my head and I have Anthony's voice over my shoulder, saying you can do this today.

I think it's about adding value, which resonates with people instead of it being, buy, buy, buy. I see people saying, "Look at me and my entrepreneur life," and I think, I don't know many entrepreneurs who are talking about their entrepreneurial life. They're working hard at their job. I never called myself an entrepreneur, I call myself a business owner.

A: *Back to what you said about Shark Tank, "They think I only have to work for five years and then cash out." They equate it to the definition of entrepreneur. We know it as being a business owner and grinding it out.*

J: For years and years, and you might not ever catch up. When I was bought out, I wasn't expecting the buyout. I wasn't shopping around. It just kind of happened.

79

A: *You said something earlier, you are able to be in different venues. You're a planner, aren't you? You build business plans and strategies? Where did this come from?*

J: I don't know. I had the business plan for Beauty Bar and another one for Pride and Glory. They took a lot of time to build out. I'm a planner. I always like to write things out because once you write them out, and you map them out, you see them more visually and you know the plan better than anyone. I always tell everybody to write it out. That way, when it is pen to paper, you see it instead of just being in your head.

A: *Let's bring it full circle for a moment and recap. The four key foundational elements you said today: plan because when a barrier comes up, you're more prepared to handle it. Be courageous. Attach a competitive and courageous spirit to barrel through the barriers. Think about the mission of others and be passionate about your goals.*

J: Absolutely. I like all that.

A: *Jennifer, you have a sister, a twin sister Danielle, and I know she's meant a lot in your life, tell us about her.*

J: I have two sisters. My little sister Brianna is a teacher of severely autistic children. She's incredible. She's such a gift. I don't know how she does it. Then I have a twin sister, Danielle who is profoundly disabled. She's been in a group home since we were two because she needs 24-hour care from a nurse.

She can't eat a lot, she can't walk, or talk, and is confined to a wheelchair. She's been a gift, the light of my life. She has shown me so many things in life I would never otherwise have been able to see. Like how the world really is.

This morning, I went for a walk and it was a beautiful morning, the sun was gorgeous, the sky was so blue. I thought, I am so freaking lucky to walk outside while some people are stuck in hospitals because they are sick. What would they do just to be outside? My sister taught me those things, the little moments of utter appreciation for what most take for granted every single day.

A: *There is such truth in your perspective. If we could break it down, be emotional for a moment about what has moved us and think about a couple of things to be grateful for, perhaps the dreams we have at night would be better.*

Jennifer, you emanate beauty from the inside out and you are truly one of those leaders who makes everyone better and the environments around her better. It has been an honor having you on the show today.

J: Thank you.

Passion and Possibility

*Living with
passion aligns
achievement with
potential. The
result is dreams
turning into
reality.*

Past choices, the responsibility of family, the day to day monotony of work, take their toll and before we know it, we have forgotten what passion feels like, let alone what we are passionate about.

Passion is like a fire deep inside of us, driving us forward, even when we are too tired take one more step. It consumes us from the minute we open our eyes until we close them again. We are driven to succeed even when it looks like there is no hope of success. At these times, when things look bleak and dark, passion stops us from throwing in the towel.

Heroes in stories are passionate about their purpose, their journey, or their moral compass. They find other ways to achieve their quest, no matter their opponent or barrier.

Be the Hero of Your Story!

What Jennifer Walsh Taught Us

Do not let the limited vision and fears of others keep you from your passion. If you want something, go after it one hundred and ten percent. They will still love you and still be there to support you, even if they do not understand what you are trying to do.

Make a difference in the world. When you are passionate about your vision, you will work hard to see it blossom no matter what happens in your life. Sometimes your passion will grow into other adventures you never imagined.

When it feels as though life may be falling apart, keep your head up, believe things are happening for a reason, and don't let the stress show. Strength comes from both courage and passion and is contagious. The combination will move you forward.

When there is enthusiasm in what we do it pushes us to realize our dreams. The only way we can understand our passion is by stopping, living in the moment, and discovering the reason we do what we do. When we embrace and own that, we have the right attitude to weather any storm.

With passion we can find the courage to move forward.

Our wonderful guests have inspired us to Push the Possible, no matter where we are in life.

86

Be Better with Passion

People can make a living doing something they're not passionate about. It is done all the time. If you feel as though you are living in a rut, with a mindless routine, then you've lost your way and your passion. When you are living a life without purpose, vision, or a mission you believe in, you may be living below your potential.

The trick is aligning yourself to your passion in your everyday activities and then doing the best you can, no matter what. If you care about what you do there is a fire lit deep inside you, which drives you forward and won't let you quit. When what you do at work every day has a purpose you are excited about, you will want to complete every task knowing each one is a part of building something bigger than yourself.

I am passionate about what I do each day and it gives me the energy I need to keep moving forward, even when things are difficult. When you are enthusiastic you will motivate others, who will gravitate toward you and want to share in your vision. Passion is infectious.

When I worked in construction, every nail I hammered, every hole I dug, everything I did helped to build the building, a building which will be there long after I am gone. Hundreds of years ago, it took three lifetimes for craftsmen to build cathedrals. Today, you can go and see their work, their legacy, and their purpose in history. Passion lies within their craftsmanship. It lies in the purpose of what we do and why we do it. If what you do every day does not align with your values, your personal beliefs, and mission in life, you may need to make a change.

Restructure to Align with Your Passion

You can align your position within a company with your passion by asking to take on different tasks. Say you are an account executive and there is an opportunity to help a project manager in a completely different department. By asking if you can help while continuing to complete your daily tasks, you will increase your skill set, show others you are willing to learn, and build connections with others in the organization. This is how a lot of my opportunities came to me because I was willing to put myself in a constant state of learning by asking how I could help someone else.

If you do this enough, you will learn faster than most people in the company and will be known as the kind of individual whom they can seek-out for help. People want to be around those who want to learn, who are positive, and who are not afraid to try something new.

Let's take Sharon for example, she started out in the investment industry as an administrative assistant pushing paper, answering phones, and data entry. This was before computers talked to each other and most everything was done using paper and pen and then manually entered into databases for reporting purposes. Now, Sharon worked hard and took on every task handed to her, even though she was not detail oriented and found the job boring. She could have done one of two things, quit or worked hard to learn her job and then take the initiative to learn other tasks in the office. She did the latter and expanded her skill set to grow into a position which challenged her. The first thing she did was take the necessary courses to become licensed in the industry so she could help the sales assistant make sales calls, organize seminars, and make appointments. When the sales assistant quit, Sharon took the initiative to call the clients to book appointments, all while continuing to complete the administrative tasks of her position to the best of her limited administrative talents.

After a year, Sharon decided to move to the city and her boss helped her find a new position as a sales assistant in a sister Brokerage Firm, which meant more courses for her to expand her certifications. She wasn't content making calls to sell stocks and push paper, she wanted to do more, so she took on the fundamental trading research tasks and marketing initiatives.

Over the next few years, she worked in various sales and marketing roles for other investment advisors, spent time in the capital markets department learning about how to take a company public, and kept taking the necessary licensing courses. Soon, she was the highest paid sales / marketing assistant in the office because she took the risk of aligning her income with an investment advisor's commission instead of a base salary. She was able to do this because she was a valuable asset with administrative, sales, research, capital markets, and marketing skills, which she purposefully gained on the job. She also possessed a natural strong work ethic and willingness to put in the hours to get the job done. By taking ownership of her position, she ensured tasks were done to her high standards and the clients were always happy. She saw her position as her own business, which she planned on growing into a long-term career.

Aligning Your Team with Passion

Through communication with your team you can identify each team member's passion and strength. When we put people into roles they are passionate about they will naturally produce better results because they love what they are doing. As leaders we can help people discover their passions by giving them the opportunity to try different roles. Talk to your people and discover if they know which tasks they excel at and which ones they struggle to complete. Then when you are looking for new team members you can seek out the ones who are passionate about the tasks existing team members find frustrating.

In a sales department there are people who are naturally gifted in roles. Some people love finding leads, networking, and hunting out new opportunities. Other people are fantastic closers and cannot wait until they can seal another deal because negotiating is a game to them. There are those who love to nurture accounts and spend time with clients to provide amazing service. Then there are the supporters, the team members who live to organize and make sure everything is done right. When you have the right people on your team focused on the tasks they are enthusiastic about, magic can happen.

The trick is finding the right people who are passionate about what they do and keeping the lines of communication open to understand where the gaps are and how to best support the team in their goals.

Grow Your Position

Assess your teammate's strengths and weaknesses: which tasks do they love doing? Perhaps as a group you can all find a win-win solution to help the team get ahead by tapping into everyone's passions. If you are unable to initiate communication within your team to restructure task assignment within your organization, ensure you volunteer for those jobs you enjoy doing, even if it means unpaid overtime. When you are debriefing your manager about the project, be passionate when telling the story of completing the tasks you love to do. As you do this, your manager and others will come to you to complete these tasks because you have established yourself as the 'Go to Person.'

Take Rick for example. For two decades Rick loved working independently as a logging truck driver before he was laid off and had to find a new position in a small town with limited options. Due to his reputation as a hard worker and his community connections, he was able to secure a position as a laborer in the city works department who was the only person licensed to drive the big vehicles to remove snow, dirt, and dig the holes with a backhoe. He was in his late forties, with a grade eight education, starting over at the bottom, digging ditches in a new structured, unionized, team environment.

He lived up to his hardworking reputation so the municipality asked him to take courses to operate the sewage plant and the waterworks building. Problem was, Rick went to school when teachers were encouraged to hit and shame students who didn't learn the right way. Every day the teachers beat him and told him he was too stupid to learn anything and for over thirty years, he'd never set foot in a classroom or read anything if he could help it. The idea of taking a course in his late forties caused major anxiety. He could have said "no," and remained digging ditches, driving graders and dump trucks. After all, he was the only one licensed to run the big trucks and it was a union job, and therefore, he was securely employed for the foreseeable future. However, he didn't like the idea of not being useful and limited to tasks he did not find challenging, so, he took on the terrifying challenge and completed the necessary courses. Rick became the best at what he did. Soon his bosses were calling him after hours to ask him how to fix something at one of the plants. Even after he retired, they asked him to come in to help train the new guys because he was their 'expert' in everything he did, which was everything in his department.

Anyone can rise to the challenge and do what is necessary to obtain a new inspiring position and then become the best at it. I did, Sharon, Rick, Caryn, Kim, and so many others have and you can too. Do not wait for permission or ask someone what to do, just figure it out. Analyze your team to discover the gaps and then volunteer to either take on new tasks or take the necessary courses to become certified to do those tasks. If you see a job that needs doing, grab it. Don't sit on your phone or computer looking for the next pair of shoes you want to buy. If you want to rise to the top, if you want opportunities to open up for you, if you want to be the best, then pick up the ball, move beyond your scope, ask for help, and learn how to do it as you go.

The Right Attitude

Jennifer went through a major upset. She was forced to sell her company, close locations, move, and get divorced. When both her personal and professional life changed, she lost her identity and needed to reinvent herself. She did not give up and in the turmoil, she knew she was better off than others because she could go to the park where she discovered a new passion.

She is a consummate optimist and a comeback artist who believes she can come back from anything. People like her know things can always be worse and have an attitude of gratitude, even in the face of adversity. They pull through because they are grounded and when things go sideways for them, they bend, they do not break. Their lives can hit rough patches, potholes, and the odd sink hole, however they know, these things make the journey memorable, interesting, and an adventure.

The perfect trips you take are boring stories to tell compared to the trips where disaster strikes. Sure, at the time it is an inconvenience to be stuck in an airport for three days but the story you get to tell will be much more interesting, especially if you make an adventure out of it by exploring and talking to other stranded passengers.

When you live your life with passion and purpose, you do not give up. You reassess and find solutions you can live with. You keep going because the fire deep inside you will not let you quit.

Transformations

In life and in business we often focus on our transformation. Can a team utilize a new consultative science? Can professionals who have decades of routine find the energy and drive to learn new organizational models? Can a mother who dedicated years to her family recreate herself by applying her intellect and talents in a new direction? What about the personal transformation of someone who looks in the mirror and decides poor fitness is no longer acceptable?

Transformation, when embraced and applied, is the intersection of dedication and inspiration. It opens the portal to personal potential and then staying in a comfort zone is undesirable. It is the catalyst to re-engineer our core competencies. When our loved ones observe what we have transformed into, we become their role model to motivate their own evolution. A mother who morphs into a healthier, more fit person becomes a positive role model to her children.

Let's explore the elements of transformation:

1) Envision your desired outcome

2) Build a detailed personal strategic plan for execution

3) List the actions and tasks associated with the transformation

4) Build a calendar of accountability and implementation

Others may question and doubt your resolve to transform because it calls into question their own personal ability to enter a transformational state. Do not allow their doubts to cloud your resolve because your success might be the one thing they need.

Your Image Matters

Jennifer Walsh has a wonderful beauty blog and she says, beauty comes down to health and our energy. Energy is a sustainable and renewable resource. You need energy to get through tough storms and the better your health, the better your energy, the tougher the storms you can weather.

Image is about how you feel about yourself; not what others see. Attention to your personal hygiene, your clothes, your fitness, your nails, even the shine of your shoes, are your personal brochure. We know that if we are not taking care of ourselves physically and mentally, when we look in the mirror, we see a mess, and are already defeated. If we are not happy with who we are inside and out, it will manifest in everything we do and we will produce at a lower potential because we will have less energy.

Image isn't about flash. You don't need an expensive wardrobe or high-end car. Image is about respecting ourselves enough to self-care. If we do that with dedication, others will trust us to take care of them. Our success is affected by how we feel in our own skin, which is 100% reflected in our image.

Look at Joanne for example. Joanne was married to a demanding man, a mom of two busy kids, and worked full time. She was so overwhelmed taking care of everyone else she had no energy to take care of herself. She spent all of her money on her kids with few resources left for her own wellbeing and wardrobe. One only had to look at her to see she was exhausted and over-burdened.

Then she lost her job.

Joanne immediately started looking for a new position and her resume provided her with many opportunities to interview because she was skilled and accomplished. Unfortunately, she didn't present well; didn't own any updated professional clothes or makeup, and her hair had been in a ponytail for almost a decade.

Without money to improve her appearance and no clue how to take care of herself, she failed to impress interviewers. The more she was rejected the worse things got for her and her self-worth suffered because she believed others didn't value her. People shied away from her negative energy and before she knew it, she was an unemployed, divorced, single mom, with no money, no prospects, and no support.

Through taking a serious look in the mirror, both physically and emotionally, she took initiative and sought out resources. Joanne was able to find help through a government agency who provided her with access to professional clothes, grooming experts, and an appointment with the local beauty school. It took time and a lot of effort but, she was able to start taking better care of herself, which resulted in more positive energy. With her newfound confidence and positive attitude, she was able to secure a customer service position with a great company.

Image isn't about how other's treat us or see us. I don't care what other people think about me. You may think what other's think of you is important to your self-esteem or self-worth. Their opinion of you is fool's gold, it isn't rare, it isn't real, and it has no value. The real gold is what we think, it is our relationship with ourselves. Our strength, confidence, and potential come from how we view ourselves, not from what others say or think about us. If you measure your value by what others think, you will not be able to weather a storm if their attention is elsewhere or you misinterpret how they value you.

When we take care of ourselves, we feel happier, more confident, and better put together. Even the smallest act of self-care can make an impact on shifting our energy and confidence. When we eat healthy, exercise regularly, and take care of our mental health, we feel happier about ourselves. The more we like ourselves, the better the chance we have of succeeding because when you fill your stores with real gold, your value to those around you will be evident and you won't care about those who don't value you.

Be Authentic, Not Counterfeit

On a Sunday, when you are tired and don't want to shine your shoes, take an hour to shine your shoes. Do something to prepare your uniform for the week so you will look and feel your best to be ready to compete. Success is ninety percent preparation. When you take care of the details, like shining your shoes, it makes an impression on yourself and those around you. You are saying "I am worth it."

You don't have to dress conservatively to be successful. Unless your place of work has issued company uniforms or a dress code, your uniform is whatever you chose to make it, as long as it fits within your company or industry's requirements. Personally, I don't care if people have tattoos or body piercings, however, be authentic in your choices and realistic about what is appropriate. Don't say you are dressing to be anti-establishment or anti-corporate when you have to interact with the people in your office and industry.

You won't be taken seriously if you have a punk rocker image in a formal business environment. The same can be said if you dress in a suit but work in the punk rock industry. Dress appropriately and be authentic to your environment, who you are and your personality.

Fake it 'til You Make It.

I'm not a big not a big fan of fakery. Faking it is just an excuse to not to prepare for tasks and you expect people to hand you responsibility without working to earn it. If you fake it, you won't be able to meet the expectations of those who have a vested interest in the outcome. If you adopt an image, talk the talk, but cannot walk the walk, you will fail, and your reputation will suffer.

If you prepare for tasks by doing the work or research ahead of time, you won't have to fake it. If you fake it 'til you make it, you are going to end up promising to do tasks you are either ill equipped or unqualified to handle, which ultimately hurts your entire team. There is a difference between expanding your skill set and faking expertise. If you want to expand, be honest about what you can do, learn from those who have done it before and ask for help when you get stuck.

> *Those who have self-respect will always outlast you because they're doing the hard stuff, taking care of the details, and doing what is necessary to succeed, even when they don't want to.*

Push Your Possible

Passion and Possibility

This is the part of the book where you dive deeply into the concepts to form your own opinions, make plans, and set goals.

I encourage you to mark up the pages and make this book a resource for your life journey.

Want to share your thoughts with me on social media? Tag me in your Twitter or LinkedIn post and use the hashtag, #PushersofPossible.

Your Values

What are your core values; those values which define you as a person?

5. _____

4. _____

3. _____

2. _____

1. _____

What do these core values say about you?

Find your Passion

What are your top five favorite things in the world? Think of hobbies, collections, physical and leisure activities.

5.

4.

3.

2.

1.

Think over these five things. What do they have in common? Why did you choose these five? How do they make you feel? Why do they stand out from the others?

Find Your Passion

What are you talking about when you feel passionate and animated?

What issues concern you and why?

Passion at Work

What is the purpose of the company you work for?

Is it a purpose you are passionate about? _____Yes _____No

How does your position work toward this purpose?

There are things about any job you can enjoy. What aspects of your job or position do you enjoy?

Passion at Work

If you believe you can restructure your position or move into another one, who do you need to talk to and what would you say?

Are there skills, courses, certificates you are missing? Where can you obtain the necessary requirements?

Can you use outside resources to help you? An assistant, technology, a networking contact.

Passion at Work

Can you work with your manager and team to restructure your position to move toward your passion?

Which people do you think have the best job in the world and why?

Transitioning

What do you want your life to be like? What would you change right now?

Envision yourself having made the change. What do you look and feel like? What are people saying about the 'New You?'

Plan of Action

Make a plan of action to move toward the new you.

What are your objectives, actions, and related tasks?

When you clearly communicate a vision, others will make the climb, and together you will see the view overlooking greatness.

Roots of Leadership
Barry Beck

Serial entrepreneur, Barry Beck, discusses his successes and strategies as a leader and innovator. Before starting Bluemercury with his wife Marla, he had three successful business ventures. Bluemercury is credited with putting a dent in the cosmetic universe and disrupting mainstream retail. Macy's acquired the company and lends its resources to the innovative retailer.

Barry credits his Personal Board of Directors for challenging him to strive for more. He explains that he always had a drive to succeed and thinks his leadership and entrepreneurial qualities are a mix of both nature and nurture. During this episode of the Roots of Leadership, Barry discusses the most important characteristics of a leader, when the best business decisions are made, and also shares advice he received from Bill Gates.

The Interview

A: *This is Anthony Gruppo, welcome to today's episode of the Roots of Leadership. I'm excited to have Barry Beck, a Co-Founder and Chief Operating Officer of Bluemercury Inc., in the studio today. Barry, Welcome to the show.*

B: Thank you for having me.

A: *I'm looking forward to this Barry. You and I have dined a few times socially, however, until I did more research for this podcast, I had no idea about the depth and expanse of the leadership you possess. A lot of people know about Bluemercury. You started it as a young man with an entrepreneurial mindset. What's the first memory you have of being an entrepreneur?*

B: I've always wanted to be an entrepreneur.

My father instilled the idea in me when I was nine or ten years old, he called me into the den and said, "You can be anything in the world you want to be, as long as you own it." I think from that moment on, I wanted to be an entrepreneur and start a company of my own.

I love entrepreneur stories. I like Salesforce.com founder, Marc Benioff's story. He started his first company in junior high school and sold it when he was in college. Afterward, he went to work at Oracle, left, and started Salesforce. Now he has bought Time magazine.

His story grabbed my attention because his story is similar to my own. I started as a young entrepreneur shoveling snow in my neighborhood. However, I think the difference between me and everyone else who starts a business, like shoveling snow at a young age, is that I had contracts with every home in the neighborhood and would give them up to a 20% loyalty discount. I then parlayed it into a landscaping business once the snow melted. I learned how to upscale at a young age and am always looking for the next big thing.

I started by charging $20 a driveway, added washing cars for $100 a car, then I had the idea of residential window washing where I could get $300 or $400 a house. I could do five houses a day and all of a sudden, I'm making $2,000 a day. I was building larger businesses when I was still in high school. Then in college, I started a company with my brother called Tower Systems, Inc., which became US Maintenance Company, now part of the Fortune 500 company, Emcor. After selling Tower Systems, I started Bluemercury.

A: *Let's talk for a minute about some of the things driving you. In an interview you said you didn't feel fulfilled at Tower Systems; you weren't as happy as you could be. However, you were doing great, it was a great company that was doing exceptionally well. What was the trigger for Barry Beck to say, "This isn't it," because that would be 'IT' for a lot of people. Barry why wasn't it - 'IT' - for you?*

B: I think everyone in life always reaches new plateaus. A friend of mine who is an art collector, said, "I'll never buy a piece of art worth more than x." Then another advisor says, "Oh no, you'll reach new plateaus and continue to reach new plateaus and new realizations."

As new things come along, you realize hey, this is the next thing I want. Each plateau has you looking around for the next challenge, which is another step toward bigger things.

When I was running Tower Systems, I was very successful, wildly successful. It had become a national business. Ultimately, we became the Kleenex tissue of our industry and I was making a lot of money. It was very financially rewarding, but it was also a very difficult business. One day, I called my brother in Washington, DC, and I said, "I'm not fully satisfied" and his response was, "I want you to put your bank account statement under your pillow, and through osmosis each night, you'll become happy." I tried that, obviously figuratively speaking. I tried being happy with just the money, but it lasted only so long. Ultimately, I began to have an itch for something new, something more fulfilling. This was at the time of the internet boom and it led me to Bluemercury.

A: *Bluemercury, the work you and your wife Marla did revolutionized the business. You came in as an outsider. Why is an outsider coming into the cosmetics industry so amazingly successful over established companies in the industry?*

B: Generally speaking, the very nature of innovation. There are two concepts; there's innovation disruption, and there's globalization. Globalization is merely taking best practices global. We can take any business, be it insurance, or cosmetics, and we roll it out around the world and improve the processes.

That's globalization.

True innovation comes from a few people in a small room, away from a big company, being forced to innovate, and disrupt, because they must for survival. It is through the need for survival where new ideas are born, like, The Facebook, which ultimately became just Facebook.

For a long time, I didn't understand why Google didn't just make Facebook and the answer is, they couldn't. It was the very fact that Zuckerberg and his crew were on their own, separate from a big company, which enabled an innovative company to form.

A: *When you think about Bluemercury, which you founded in 1999, when you sold it to Macy's, you could have walked away. You could have said "Okay on to the next big thing," but you stayed with Bluemercury as a COO, responsible for strategic planning, with all kinds of data analysis. Why did you stay when you could have gone anywhere?*

B: I think the easy answer is, I'm in the beauty business. When I first started the company, I asked a senior manager at Barney's New York to give me one word of advice and he said to me, "When the moments get tense, and they eventually will, and you're really stressed, you're running out of cash and there are lots of problems going on in your business, remember, you sell lipstick for a living, you're not curing cancer, you're not doing heart surgery."

I have the great fortune to be in the fashion and beauty industry. It's an amazing industry. I'm meeting great entrepreneurs and there is so much innovation going on and lots of product proliferation. I think one of the interesting things is our parent company, Macy's, has allowed us to swim in our own lane and we continue to learn from each other. I've been able to sell my cake and eat it too, which is, I'm able to operate my own company independently from the mothership, but with a set of resources I really never could have even imagined as a standalone venture.

A: *I want to recap four things you said today. So far, we have talked about owning it, new plateaus, the nature of innovation, and when moments get tense. A lot of leaders face those moments. It doesn't matter if you are a CEO of an insurance company or the COO of a company like Bluemercury, you have to be tough. What makes you tough? Because you have a toughness. Where does it come from?*

B: I'm a Philly boy.

A: *Yes, we are both Eagles fans. The crowd needs to know I grew up in Lehigh Valley and Barry is from Philadelphia.*

B: People ask me, what does it mean to have the right stuff? The right stuff is intestinal fortitude. Having the ability to go through the hard times. Starting a business, as you know, is akin to eating glass at times. It's going to be hard. Sometimes I tell people, if starting your company is too easy, you're probably doing it wrong. This is part of the innovation process.

I think any great leader has four key traits. One is strength. Two is courage. I would say three is wisdom, and the fourth, is a certain amount of charisma. To a lesser extent, you need some intelligence. The reason is, you need to have the strength to change industries. If you can change them, you have to have the courage to face the things you can't change, and the wisdom to know the difference between the two, then to get your teams to follow, you have to have charisma. Plus, you need to have some smarts, but to a lesser extent. It's hard to define what smart is. Is it wisdom? Is it courage? Is it strength? All the above?

A: *To be successful as leaders, we have to have the four things you said: strength, courage, wisdom, and charisma. These four things are critical.*

Barry, you raised a million dollars and by the time you finished building a website and you'd spent $850,000 of it. That's a challenging moment, especially because you had to make changes and only had $150,000 left. Initially, you started off thinking this was going to be a virtual store in the online world. Then, you had to pivot on a dime and you were running out of money. Where's Barry Beck's mindset at this moment?

B: I tell entrepreneurs their best decisions are made from a position of strength and not weakness. Unfortunately, in my career, the times when I was the most flush with capital, I usually made the most mistakes. The idea of being scrappy, or doing more with less, was when I made my best decisions. At the time when the site was up and we only had $150,000 left in the bank, I went into survival mode. We had to survive.

One day, we came across an interesting little boutique in Georgetown, DC. Here we were an online cosmetics company and the problem was, we were too early. Sometimes being one of the first ones into a new industry is the wrong decision. It's about timing. The technology was great, but it was tantamount to giving a Tesla to the Romans. They'd say, "That's really cool, but what do we do with this thing?" In 1999, no one was shopping online. The only people who were buying from my website in 1999 were my competitors to see what I was up to. We knew we needed to change what we were doing. Changing what you're doing in the middle of operating your business is called a pivot, the necessary next step, and we pivoted to a blended strategy. Incidentally, our investors hated the idea. They wanted a pure internet business, to stay with what they thought was the core business.

A lot of people will say, "Well, what does your board of directors think about this?" The answer is, it's all about management and the management has to know what's going on. I took the blended idea to the board and said, "We have to pivot, we have to buy the brick-n-mortar stores." Ultimately, they said if you want to buy stores, buy them on your own, you can't buy them with our money. My wife and I bought the stores and then ended up merging the businesses, with the board's permission. My ownership shot up to over 90% of the overall business. We were lucky it worked out. It could have gone the other way.

A: *Barry, you said how sad it makes you to watch people start a business intent on selling it immediately, I think your words were, "Build a great company." When you think about a level of greatness, what's greatness to you? How do you define it?*

B: I think it's different in every business because there are so many different types. At Bluemercury it was always about the Warren Buffett way of building a consumer monopoly.

I always wanted to build a business where I had brands my clients would come in to buy year, after year, after year, because they loved them. The products worked and they couldn't live without them. This was something really important to me. We built a moat of convenience around our clients by building stores near where they lived and worked. We became an upscale drugstore, where people could buy shampoo, shaving cream, shower gel, toothpaste, deodorant, and we created a set of annuity products. An annuity product is a product our clients come in to buy year-after-year, because they work, and clients can't live without them. This is the secret of success for us.

To a smaller degree, I love seeing our Bluemercury shopping bags around New York City. I'll be spending today in the New York area, in Manhattan, and I love seeing our bags running around.

A: *I was at an event at the Midtown Hilton and as I'm walking up to the building, there's Bluemercury. I get back to Montclair, I'm walking down through the little town and there is Bluemercury. I'm seeing your stores. I'm seeing them in Midtown. I'm seeing them in Montclair. What an amazing achievement you and Marla have accomplished. How do you see Barry Beck now? What still inspires you?*

B: I would say a few things. One is, I don't take myself too seriously. I don't live my life precariously. I realize I didn't get here on my own and it wasn't easy. It took Bluemercury fifteen years to become an overnight success. It didn't happen overnight. It took a lot of hard work.

For now, I've entered a sort of the benevolent phase of my life. We're giving back to entrepreneurship and social innovation by setting up the Beck Fellowship for Entrepreneurs at Cornell

118

University. I'm helping young entrepreneurs start their businesses by defraying the cost of entrepreneurship. We pay them an hourly wage when they are on school break, so they don't have to go work and try to pay back their student loans and they can focus on building great businesses.

I grew up in a tough household. Once, I said to my brother "I am successful." My brother says, "No you're not. You know Steven Spielberg made Jaws when he was twenty-three. That's successful." It was a pretty high bar, but I think one of his messages to me was, never compare down. It's all about comparing up. I always compare up. I know there are still cities in America without a Bluemercury store. I've got a lot of work to do and have a long runway in front of me. More products, more categories to disrupt, and more stores, there is a lot of work for me to do.

A: *I want to recap because you pack a lot into your comments. I want to break it down for the listeners.*

Don't take yourself too seriously. Work to give back. Don't compare down. Blend it all with strength, courage, wisdom and charisma. Be able to pivot in life when you have to.

When you think about what you've experienced and what you have seen since you were at Cornell, think about when you were getting ready to graduate and you were already making a million dollars. How did you make a million dollars in college?

B: I was a scrappy young entrepreneur. This was something which was instilled in me from a young age. My father's father instilled it in me from a young age. My paternal Grandfather died when he was a very young man and my mother came from a wealthy family. My father said, "I'd rather be poor than work for my father-in-law." We weren't really poor, we weren't rich either, we were very middle class, lower middle class. I had no capital to start a business, still, I kept taking the steps, looking to operate a business at scale, and trying to grow.

I was already making one hundred thousand dollars my senior year of high school, which at the time was more than most lawyers and doctors were making. One day, I was with my brother and a friend when we came across an office building. We saw a guy working there and asked, "What do you do?" He says, "I take care of this office park and do integrated maintenance services here." I said, "Well, how much do you make?" Remember, I was making $100,000, he made $400,000, and BOOM, a light bulb went off in my head - "Oh, there's the next step." We looked at what he was doing, we innovated and disrupted the entire chain store maintenance industry.

A: *You talk about disrupting an entire industry. You became a major disruptor and you're how old at this point in your story?*

B: I'm twenty.

I think it's possible to be disruptive at any age. I don't have the energy I had then, the indefatigable energy you have when you're young, but I still want to disrupt my industry. I tell young entrepreneurs, "You make the bed you sleep in for the rest of your life between the ages of twenty and thirty." I'm starting new businesses all the time and have enough ideas for five lifetimes. I never was on a traditional path. I was never going to graduate school; I was never going to go to a J-O-B. I never interviewed on college campuses. It wasn't for me. In fact, when I started to work at Macy's, they wanted me to do an assessment and review. I told the guy who wanted to do my assessment, "I'd never been on a job interview in my life before and I'd never had a job review. I don't know what it's like." I was about starting companies, not working for them.

A: *A lot of people in the world are jumping through these human resources hoops, personality assessments, interview processes, and performance reviews. I wonder sometimes, if everyone starts to get stuck in the trap of expectations, all because they took a test and were given a profile about their energy level, their acumen, and their talents.*

Instead of just playing the game a little loose, do you think people are playing the game too tight?

B: Entrepreneurs and disruptors are everywhere. The disruptors and entrepreneurs whom I respect and admire are Steve Jobs because he broke the rules, Jeff Bezos because he just went out there and solved a problem, and Phil Knight from Nike because he was the one who said, "Just do it."

Look at Steve Jobs. He created the iPhone, which really broke all the rules because it changed how we use our phones, listen to music, and how we take taxis. He changed the very fabric of how we live our lives.

I recently heard Jeff Bezos from Amazon say, "Every great decision I made in my life was not done through analysis, it was all gut instinct."

Once I met a really bright business manager who went to Harvard Business School. He turned to me one time and said, "Barry, you can't make this decision this way, there's no such thing as instinct." And I said, "Well, instinct is just pattern recognition."

Jeff Bezos was a problem solver who used instinct to disrupt how people shop. I always say, "No problem, no solution, no company." You have to be out there solving problems and be able to think outside the box.

Look at Phil Knight and his "Just do it" slogan. He just jumped into the sneaker business. He never would have seen the opportunity if he hadn't started out by selling other people's sneakers first.

A: *I don't remember who the individual was whom you spoke to, but you were starting a new adventure and you said, "Ask Bill Gates what he thinks." Bill Gates response to you was, "There are no paper clips." What does that mean?*

B: A good friend of mine went to Harvard with Bill Gates and Steve Ballmer. Steve, who is now CEO at Ameritas of Microsoft, is the sole investor in my friend's new company. We were going to start a new company and I told my friend, "Go ask Bill Gates to give me one piece of advice." He went to see Bill and Bill said, "Tell Barry Beck, 'no more paper clips.' " That was it. I pushed it back to him when we were having lunch, I said, "Call Bill and ask him, what does 'no more paper clips mean?' " Bill just said, "Barry, at your age it's better to start with a small fledgling business because it's hard to start from zero."

A: *I've heard you say this before. Your advice has always been, start something by buying an existing company, which you did. Bluemercury was an existing business.*

B: It was EF/FX and it wasn't working. We bought it and used that to change the industry. Some of America's greatest businesses started like that. I don't know if the listeners have heard of a company called Il Giornale. It was a four-store coffee chain owned by Howard Schultz, who bought Starbucks in 1984, and the rest is history. A lot of people don't know who Starbuck was - he is a character in the novel Moby Dick.

A: *Barry, when you think back, have you faced a challenge where you are in the middle of solving a problem and it starts to break down or feel insurmountable? It just felt like, this might be the one Barry is going to struggle with.*

B: I think it was said best by Benjamin Franklin who said, "If your outflow is greater than your intake, your upkeep will result in your downfall." So for me, one of the things I learned along the way with my first two national companies, both of which came close to insolvency - twice, is cash flow is the lifeblood of every business. You see so many different industries in the internet industry in tech and there is now this new explosion in the cannabis industry. All these companies are growing without cash flow, which generally ends badly.

A: *No matter how innovative the product, how great the system, or how much a disruptor, without cash flow, you cannot sustain.*

B: Number one, it's important to remember that the first year is the hardest. If you think about the first year in terms of software, going from version 0 to version 1 - the thing is very buggy. Think of your iPhone going from version 1 to version 2, also buggy, but nothing like version 0 to 1. It's important to stay the course. You may have to sprint your first year, but you'll ease into the marathon, given enough time. The second part of my message the listeners need to take away from this interview would be DROM, which means don't run out of money, because when you run out of money it's, 'Game Over.'

I try to explain this to my eleven-year-old son who started multiple businesses already by selling stuff at school and online. I tell him, in the old days we used to play a game called Pac Man. You'd get a bag of quarters and go down to the arcade. You'd put quarters into the machine to play the game and when you ran out of money, it was 'Game Over,' and you'd go home.

A: *What does he say to his dad? What does this young entrepreneur at age eleven, who is already selling online, say to his dad?*

B: He doesn't take me too seriously. I'm just Dad. I saw a great interview with a famous Rock-and-Roll star who said, "I'm just not cool to them." Mick Jagger comes home to his kids. He's not cool. He's just dad. I don't know if my son listens to me that much. We're partners in business. I help him. We've gotten into a 3D printing business together and he's seen some success with it. I've helped fund some of his ventures and they are all cash flow positive. At eleven-years-old I think he's got more Instagram followers than Bluemercury.

A: *Let's go back to Bluemercury for a moment. This is not your average cosmetic business, it's way above average. I'm going to try to paraphrase something I heard you say about building new products. You said a lot of the products used in the industry had ingredients you would never use in your products. You had the lab work on healthier, cleaner, and ecologically better formulas, which made the customer experience different. Where did this idea come from? This was a game-changer. This put Bluemercury on the map and made it magnificent. Where did the idea come from?*

B: It's interesting. It's the big picture. I would say in any large disruption, people ultimately get hurt. The taxi cab drivers hate Uber because, in this large disruption, the cabbies are getting hurt since they resisted the change. There's a sort of natural lethargy in every industry to keep doing things the same way.

That's how things are.

When we started Bluemercury, all of the so-called experts told us we were out of our minds. We had no idea how the business worked. It didn't make any sense. People were happy with the products fifteen years ago and ninety percent of all cosmetics were purchased at department stores. The problem was with those current product offerings was the products either didn't work, they smelled bad, or the packaging was terrible. So, we set out on a science experiment to stabilize the Vitamin C we wanted to deliver into the skin, yet we had no way of doing this because it kept degrading. Vitamin C turns brown and degrades over time.

Of course, all the laboratories told me everything I wanted to accomplish with natural ingredients couldn't be done. We created a list of a hundred banned ingredients, those things we wouldn't put into our products like parabens, sulfates, and factions. Those who were helping me design the products didn't believe they would be successful, however, three years later, it was a whole new entrepreneurial venture. We launched M61 powerful skincare, which was a runaway success and the number one selling skincare line at Bluemercury. Our clients are very sophisticated. How you measure success in retail is by repeat purchases, what we call calm sales growth, or like-for-like growth each year. These are the annuity products our clients come in for year after year. For instance, one of our products, Power Glow Peel, we sell one every eight seconds, so I think it really speaks for itself.

We were part of this mass disruption and are widely recognized for changing the face of mainstream beauty shopping. In terms of our products, I think after about 2008, right after the Great Recession, customers were coming into our stores looking for more natural products.

One of the reasons we've been very successful, is we are driven data junkies. We are always looking at the data and we realized there were more vegetarians in the millennial generation than any other generation in history. Our products fit their value systems.

A: *What strikes me is, you are an entrepreneur, a global strategist* *and have an attention to detail. You have a linear and global mindset, which is unusual. Did you learn it? Were you born with it? How are you able to be strategic and detail-oriented at the same time?*

B: I believe some of it is nature and some of it is nurture. I always had this drive to succeed. As you know, I grew up in a lower middle-class family. I was very tangential to my cousins, who were way more affluent than we were, and I don't think it created a chip on my shoulder, so much as it really drove me to look for autonomy. I saw this idea of autonomy, of independence, by building a company and being in control of my own destiny. It is what really drove me, and I think any successful entrepreneur who says he's only a big picture disruptor and isn't into details, is probably not telling you the truth. You have to be in the details. Ultimately, over time, you can fill in the ranks of your lieutenants, who are going to help you be in the detail. But first, you have to take care of the details.

A: *I absolutely share your thoughts on that. As a CEO of a large organization and region, I cannot be helpful to my colleagues, my leadership team, and others, if I don't know enough of the details, because when they bring me a situation, we have to talk it through. If you are too above it all, what help are you? You have to be able to solve those issues by understanding the details.*

I want to recap something because I think it's important and you're packing so much into this interview. Nature and nurture look for autonomy to control your destiny is something you said, which I will always carry with me after today. Instinct is mere pattern recognition. There are a lot of people who never gain instinct because they quit too soon. It's tough because they bail, swim to the next shiny object, and bail again. You and I know these people. What advice do you have when it's about to break you, how do you stay in the battle?

B: I found strength by creating a Personal Board of Directors around me. This has really helped me and sustained me through my darkest times. I was in a conversation with a very bright entrepreneur, and I was one hundred percent sure he was getting bad advice. He was talking to a very smart person, but it's not always about raw intellect, sometimes it's about wisdom. You know, being smart is knowing a tomato is a fruit, but wisdom is knowing not to put it in a fruit salad.

I've surrounded myself with a Personal Board of Directors who give me great advice and different perspectives. Some are great legal minds with a wise perspective, and some are smart entrepreneurs who have done it before. These are people who love me, understand me, and care about me selflessly versus, the other people who have their own agendas. It's not easy.

The first year is going to be the hardest. You have to have intestinal fortitude. It's a marathon, you may have to sprint at the beginning, but you'll settle in and get used to it.

A: *I smiled when you talked about your Personal Board of Directors because in my first book, Creating Reality, a Guide to Personal Accomplishment, which I wrote twenty years ago, it has a chapter about building a Personal of Board Directors. I can't tell you how many successful people I've talked to, some of them on the show, who have said they've built a Personal Board of*

Directors. It's critical. You said something important, "Sometimes we have people who are close to us, love us, and are fearful for us because they don't want to see us fail or get hurt, especially if it could impact them." I think what Barry and I would say to the listeners today is surround yourself with people who challenge.

B: We've talked about this already, it's all about problems, you know, no problem, no solution, no company, and it's sort of like a piece of clay. As you become a developed or seasoned executive, it's those grooves in the clay which comes from rubbing against the abrasive surfaces that make you seasoned. Someone asked me what it's like to become a seasoned executive. I said I think about it as a great steak, if it's beaten with a cleaver with salt rubbed in the wound over time, this is what makes a delicious piece of steak.

People say, Barry, you are a great and seasoned entrepreneur and I say, "I know I've taken a few lickings in my day and that's part of it." Some people don't have the intestinal fortitude and it's not for everybody. People I talk to say, "I look at what you do Barry and I could never do it." Okay, well, come join my team and I'll find a role for you. I think it's about getting the right people on the bus and then finding the right seat for them on it. Not everybody's the driver. I'm the driver of this bus. I'd rather never get on the bus, unless I am the driver.

A: *As you build your legacy through your children, your eleven-year-old is already in the business of being in business. What do you want to be remembered for Barry? This isn't about ego Barry. I'm looking at you across the table in the studio right now, two men who had to make the climb wondering what do you want to be remembered for?*

129

B: When somebody asks me what I want to pass on to my children I think of a few things. I think the most important thing is perspective. In America today, by design of our tax law, there's no such thing as dynastic wealth. I mean this. You are never going to pass it along. Even Bill Gates says he only going to leave

his kid ten million, which I think is a little rough. He is saying that with all the connections, everything you've learned in your life, it should be enough. You should be able to make it on your own, but our world is not designed, certainly in America, to be that way. I want to pass along a great perspective to my kids and a global understanding. We spend a lot of time traveling the world. We have taken our kids to some incredible places, Africa, Morocco, Laos, Cambodia, so they will understand they are part of a much broader ecosystem and community.

As far as Bluemercury goes, obviously you know we were a Harvard Business School case study. We are recognized as a company who completely disrupted the cosmetics industry, a sixty billion industry, which we fundamentally changed. It wasn't easy, but we dented the cosmetic universe and it's still working today, twenty years later. I think we are widely recognized for disrupting Main Street retail, along with companies like Starbucks. We are filling out these urban locations and suburban locations in towns where people used to shop at malls and over time the malls were no longer convenient. Malls were created for two reasons, number one convenience, and two breadth of selection. Now ultimately, you get your breadth of selection online, and malls aren't as convenient as they used to be, due to traffic from increasing populations. I think we made a fundamental change to cosmetics, a fundamental change to retail shopping in America, and then as far as my family goes, giving my kids a great perspective so they're part of a global community.

A: *Those three things are so critical Barry, thank you for sharing. You know what the global understanding is in a broad depth of how the world interacts. It has been a great honor having you on the show today, Barry.*

B: Pleasure was actually mine. Thank you for having me. It's been very enjoyable.

Innovation and
Disruption

There is nothing stopping you, except you, from reaching the biggest, scariest, most insane goals you can dream up. Do not make excuses, do not blame, others, and constantly reach for another rung on the ladder of challenge that makes you uncomfortable.

Throughout history, how we do things is constantly changing as inventors pioneer innovative technology, ideas, and processes. Being able to disrupt an industry takes a certain kind of visionary. Men like Steve Jobs, Jeff Bezos, Edison, Bell, and the Wright brothers risked everything to see their dreams become a reality. We can debate which invention was the most important to humanity and there would be no clear winner. Be it the printing press, the fax machine, the light bulb, cars, assembly lines, computers or smartphones, each one has led us to where we are today.

There are plenty of names throughout history we don't know. These are men and women who tried, failed, and for one reason or another never seemed to be the one to make history. For every iconic innovator in history, there are competitors who never rose to the top.

What does it take to be 'The One?' Why Thomas Edison over Joseph Swan, or Alexander Bell instead of Philip Reis or Hermann Ludwig Ferdinand von Helmholtz? Every innovator had competitors who fell from the annals of history class.

What makes one innovator better than the rest? Luck? Skill? Innate business acumen? Whatever the reason, those who have made life what it is today had a vision, a dream, and the audacity to disrupt the status quo. They created their own reality.

What Barry Beck Taught Us

There are entrepreneurs who were born to strike out on their own and create their own destiny through innovation and disruption. By asking people questions about what they do and how they do it, Barry Beck found new and better ways to get the job done. He was not handed success; he found it and then did the work to grow into a national company by learning as he went.

Being an effective leader takes strength, courage, wisdom, and charisma. Starting a business and growing it into a national power-house is hard work and not for everyone. If you are going to be an entrepreneur, first build a great company and then seek a lucrative deal.

Don't stop looking for the next big thing because success is subjective. Strive to be more successful by looking up to those who are more accomplished than you. Innovation comes from finding new ways to do something better and it happens when you have to do more with less.

Always be on the balls of your feet because sometimes you must pivot. Those who can change direction fast to keep up with the times or put on the brakes to wait for the marketplace to catch up will still be in business tomorrow.

People will try to protect you by saying you can't do something, or they will not be able to see a way to do it themselves, so they believe it cannot be done. Don't listen to them. Instead, develop a Personal Board of Directors to help you make better decisions and find the resources you need to grow.

Owning it Means…

'Owning it' is a mindset which says you own the outcome of your work. It means, when you invest time and resources on something which fails, you suffer a setback because you care about the outcome. When you don't own it, if something fails, it doesn't impact you because if it doesn't work, so what, it didn't hurt you. With lack of ownership, you don't feel any loss, you don't care how it affects other people, and you continue on with your day as if nothing wrong has happened, while others suffer your consequences.

People who own it have a can-do attitude, are disciplined, focused, and possess a hard-driving model. The reason you want to own your position, your tasks or your daily work, is because problems give you the courage, confidence, and the ability to take greater risks. If you own it, you will try harder to do your best because you feel affected by the outcome.

I've been sent into tough situations where if I didn't own it, or believe in it, or make it my own, I wasn't going to be successful. I have walked into rooms where everyone is struggling with performance results and they looked to me, hoping I'd be able to turn things around for them. This is a great weight as I have been doubted because those who came before me failed, people resisted change, or they believed a successful outcome was not possible. No matter where I have gone, what type of situation I walked into, fortunately there were always a few people who wanted to work with me to improve the results.

I was once faced with a business turnaround situation in Texas where it was so bad, I felt as though I was in over my head. I truly doubted I had the skill to do what was asked of me. I went into the assignment thinking, "Oh well, if things don't work out, I can always go back to where I was." That was when I realized my thinking was flawed because I believed things were going to fail and I'd already started to build my exit plan.

Instead of building an escape pod, I decided to fearlessly go forward, own the task set before me and play each day as though it were my last to drive the team toward the goal line. I realized there was no going back. It was 'get it done' or nothing. When you play a high-risk game without a net you truly own it.

If you want to own it, do not think about your job title, your specific role, or about your lack of authority. Owning it means doing your very best to get the job done. Have you ever tried to get help from someone only to be told, "That's not my job" or "I don't have the authority to help you," or worse, they out and out lie to you making promises they know they will not be able to deliver on?

Never be that person.

If you come up against a problem, find out who can help you solve it, and make certain it gets done. This could mean communicating the desired outcome to different departments, a supervisor, or the person beside you. If you want to find a solution, discover those who can work with you to find the solution to fix it.

When I worked in the construction industry, I decided I was going to shovel the most dirt. I was going to push the wheelbarrows faster. I was going to climb the scaffolds before anybody else did and I decided I was going to learn how to operate a backhoe. I owned whatever job I could, even if owning it was at the end of a shovel. I wasn't going to let the heat, the cold, or anything stop me from doing the best job I could. I owned the ground I was standing on, the hole I was punching into the earth, and the next challenge I was going to take on. I never changed that mindset. I always delivered the best I could, sought out ways to help others, and found challenges to grow my skills, my reputation, and my sphere of influence. I believe the minute you start doing only your job description, you open yourself up to limitation, disappointment and failure.

If you do the best you can, your chances of being successful are higher. Don't make excuses, such as, my supervisor did not do it right, I did not have the right geographical location, or I was sent to a place harder than somewhere else. I have been in hard places. I have worked in Erie, Pennsylvania.

Erie, Pennsylvania was a fairly depressed little town. When I told people I was going there to help turn things around, people asked me in disbelief and with scorn in their voice, "You are going to Erie, Pennsylvania? Why? It's cold. It's dreary. It's depressing. All the businesses are going downhill there."

Erie is a tremendous community. It is a charming town filled with great people who supported me. I went there to help them with the mindset that it was my ground, my shovel, my hole, and I have to tell you, we were wildly successful there.

When I was CEO of Marsh & McLennan Northeast in New York City people said, "Oh, well, you're in New York, you have every resource you can possibly have." Yes. True. But it's also a street fight every day. The best of the best play here and they'd eat me for breakfast if I let them.

No matter where I am, whether I'm in Erie Pennsylvania or New York City, it's the same mindset - I own my position.

If you are not getting the results you need, stop, ask questions, reassess, and analyze the data. Talk to people around you. Ask people you trust, "How do you think I'm doing?" or "How would you solve this problem?" Then start again.

Leaders want to work with people who help themselves to ensure success. Everyone should be able to ask leadership to clearly define roles, responsibilities, and tasks. Insist on the right tools for the job, ask questions, and obtain feedback. Sadly, most people will keep giving the status quo with their heads down hoping things will work out.

The following scenario happens all too often in my life. I assign a team a project with clearly defined goals and then something goes wrong. Instead of asking for help, they wait for someone to save them, see them, and help them because they are too scared to speak up, or worse, they are hiding the poor results hoping no one will notice. Upon review, the team says, "I'm surprised you didn't know. You are the CEO." How can I possibly know what literally hundreds of people are doing every day if they don't tell me what they are struggling with?

When something starts going sideways you need to communicate with your managers, team members, and colleagues, so adjustments can be made before the project goes completely off the rails. Too often people keep plugging away, ignoring red flags, and then they throw their hands in the air when things go wrong and say, "It is not my problem, I did my job." Then finger pointing and blaming others starts. This type of attitude and behavior is the complete opposite of an ownership mentality.

Plateaus

I've never reached a plateau. On the contrary, every ledge I've climbed to, I always thought I was balancing on one leg with one arm extended up to the next ledge. I've been blessed to be around amazing people whom I think are so much better than me and who keep me from feeling as though I've hit a plateau in my life.

Plateaus can be dangerous because if I feel as if I've arrived or reached a plateau, then I might stop reaching for the next challenge. I'll start taking myself too seriously, I'll become a legend in my own mind, and that is not somewhere I want to be.

If you do hit a plateau or feel stuck, you need to keep trying to be better every day, without making excuses. Plateaus occur because we start making excuses, we get frightened or believe we don't belong. I was booked to speak to a group in London, and as I was flying over the Atlantic, I had a confidence crack. I thought, "Who am I to be speaking to these great leaders in the United Kingdom and Ireland? What could I have to say to help them?"

When I got there, the level of engagement, the sincerity, their desire for help, inspiration, motivation, and ideas, inspired me. I realized it doesn't matter where we stand on the planet; we are all part of a global community of people who need help and are aiming to become the best versions of ourselves.

Over the weekend, while walking the streets around London where people were playing with their children, and families were simply enjoying life, I saw people who want the same things. We all want to belong, feel loved, and live the best life we possibly can.

We can strive for a plateau of humanity where we help each other and care about each other, but not a plateau of personal success. One where the people in London and the people in New York are all living the same happy lives full of love, friends and family. That is the only plateau to aspire to because it's not based on money, on success, or a title. Pushing to make the world a better place is a constant goal to strive for, one we should never become complacent in our pursuit of.

When we become too complacent, we can lose our vision, our sense of purpose, and end up stuck. Don't end up stuck. Keep reaching for the next level.

Innovation in Business

Every time I have a business scenario to fix or a life hiccup, I use my experiences, along with information from others, to find the best solution and then I Push the Possible. After I establish a baseline, I let my imagination run wild by visualizing different outcomes through creative thinking and by asking myself thought-provoking questions.

Three years ago, we installed my proprietary training model called Six Degrees of Impact at Marsh & McLennan Northeast. At the time, much of the insurance industry was very transactional and traditional, based on quotes, rates, and coverage. Client loyalty and retention suffered because of the stale transactional sales only approach. I wanted to change the way Insurance companies, their employees, and sales departments interacted with their clients and potential clients.

Six Degrees became a major disruptor because it applied a consultative science to the world of insurance and risk, which enabled our sales and service teams to acquire more business faster. The need to gain the trust and loyalty of the client became more important than the revolving door of quote price shopping. Since the new model was implemented, phenomenal results were achieved and other regions around the globe have started to hear about our success and are exploring implementation of Six Degrees.

When we implemented the Six Degrees model our goal was to help the Northeast region become more profitable, more successful for our colleagues, our community, and our clients. We didn't envision it would lead to global opportunities.

Over the three years I had been the CEO of Marsh & McLennan Agency Northeast, we modified the process, kept adding to the model, tried new things, and became more innovative in our approach. As we improved upon it, our successes further expanded, other regions began to take notice and now I lead a team of talented professionals in the UK, all because I was inventive, did more than my job description, and found the best people to be on my team.

Had we not been innovative or if we'd had a myopic view of success, we would not have been able to be disruptive and therefore, productive. We took a risk, explored new ideas, and discovered a new way of doing things. Once we started on our new course, we continually course-corrected by tweaking the system, until we exceeded our initial dream. It was hard work and everyone on the team contributed to our success.

Every industry, including yours, has stagnant models which are consistently average and open for renovation. You can disrupt your industry, as Barry Beck did with Bluemercury and Jennifer Walsh did with Beauty Bar. They found the weakest point in a competitive zone and entered it with a solution of change, which led to a whole new way of doing business in their industries.

Success is great and it's easy to tell stories of our accomplishments however, we don't always succeed. Back in the late 80s and early 90s, I built Association programs for the behavioral health care world. I started in Pennsylvania, expanded to Ohio, and New Jersey, and eventually nationally. What I was doing was innovative, was needed, and people were taking me with them into new opportunities. However, I hadn't built the resources behind me to sustain the expansion. In the end, I lost a few years of growth because I didn't wait to scale properly and kept acquiring more opportunities until I couldn't deliver promised results. This is a consistent story going back to the days of Rome when leaders would expand geographically without the logistics to get resources to the front lines.

I never made that mistake again.

When you are striking out with an innovative idea, you will stumble, fail, crash and burn at times. That's fine. That's what you are supposed to do. If you want to succeed and get over the goal line, you must take risks, make mistakes, and you have to learn to improve.

You can't give up. When an idea fails, figure out why it didn't work, talk to people, ask questions, analyze data, and correct your course. Listen to those whom you trust and be willing to throw things overboard because in the end, your failures don't matter, it is what you do after them that counts.

> *Here is something you may not know; the CEO is at the bottom of the corporate pyramid, not at the top because we rent our positions. We only own it for a short time to make it better for the next person to pick up the ball and run with it. We aren't merely builders of business, we are renovators of the organization with the sole purpose of making it better for the next person to carry the mantel of CEO.*

Push Your Possible

Innovation and Disruption

This is the part of the book where you dive deeply into the concepts to form your own opinions, make plans, and set goals.

I encourage you to mark up the pages and make this book a resource for your life journey.

Want to share your thoughts with me on social media? Tag me in your Twitter or LinkedIn post and use the hashtag, #PushersofPossible.

Innovation is an Idea

What processes are impeding growth in your industry?

Envision an outlandish solution, even if it is Sci-Fi, and describe it.

Innovation is an Idea

How would your idea make people's lives better?

What do you need to make your outlandish idea a reality?

Will You Own It?

What does owning it mean to you?

When you have had a problem within a company and the person you were dealing with owned their position and solved the problem for you, what did they do and how did you feel? Be specific.

How You Own It

When you experienced a major problem and inconvenience for where the person you were talking to didn't do anything to help, what happened and how did you feel? Be specific.

Think about the last problem you had to solve at work. How did you own or could you have owned it? Be honest with yourself.

Success will never be achieved until people seek to duplicate what you started.

Roots of Leadership
Hakikia Dubose-Wise

We are joined by Hakika Dubose-Wise, the nation's youngest female franchisor, Hakika, aka Kika, is the founder and CEO of Kika Stretch Studios, with four locations between New Jersey and New York. She has been recognized in NJBIZ, The New York Times, US News, and more!

She is a former professional dancer and actress who learned the value of a strong work ethic from her entrepreneurial mother, which enabled her to overcome the challenges she faced. Fear has met its match in Hakika Dubose-Wise, the youngest female franchisor.

The Interview

A: *This is Anthony Gruppo, Welcome to today's episode of the Roots of Leadership Podcast. This is going to be a show you do not want to miss. Today, I'm with Hakika Dubose-Wise the founder and CEO of Kika Stretch Studios. Hakika Welcome to the show.*

K: Thank you.

A: *I understand you are the youngest female franchisor in the United States.*

K: I am.

A: *Quite an amazing achievement. How did you become the youngest female franchisor in the United States?*

K: I never looked at the franchise model as something I wanted to do because it seemed scary. People told me how much of a headache it was, so I avoided it. Then, I realized, in order to allow others to purchase my business and run my business, I had to franchise. I had a little talk with myself and I just did it. Later, I learned I'm the youngest female franchisor.

A: *There is a lot of work to being a franchisor, but you are not afraid of hard work, are you?*

K: I'm not.

A: *Where does it come from? Where did you find the passion and the drive to become successful?*

K: I think I learned it from my mother's work ethic. She is a serial entrepreneur. As a kid, I shopped in Staples with her and was on her typewriter from a very young age smelling the paper. The fresh smell of notebooks and writing always appealed to me.

A: *We already have something in common because I love the smell of fresh textbooks. Kika where did the genius for your business come from?*

K: I went to Montclair State and studied dance. At my graduation I started crying because I realized I studied dance for four years and thought, "What am I going to do now?" There was no guidance. There was no plan for the future after graduating.

I started acting and dancing professionally, in TV and film, however, once I realized I had to play a role, I felt like it was not enough for me. I wanted to control my own time. When I decided to stop dancing, I wanted to keep my physical flexibility, so I stretched certain body parts in a certain sequence. I asked myself, "What if I did this to other people, would it work for them too?" The answer was, "Yes." I decided to stretch clients out of a small gym in Bloomfield, where I lived, and people loved it. I developed a method based on my routine.

A: *There is a big difference between having a good idea, your stretch model, and building a business. You have started to build a very successful business with four studios. I meet a lot of people who have good ideas, but never actualize them.*

What would you share with the listeners? What made your idea to dream a reality?

K: People came to me and said, they wanted to do this or that, and I asked them, "What's stopping you?" Of course, it's fear. Fear of the unknown. The unknown is a scary place, but it is also a place of greatness and happiness when you get through the unknown to your goal. We don't really know what's going to happen in life, it's unknown, but you have to take a chance. For me, not taking a chance means that I'm stuck. I can feel claustrophobic in my life and in my goals if I'm not moving forward. One day, I asked myself, why do I keep setting goals and I realized it was because I have to grow. I need to grow.

A: *I tell people, "Do not be afraid to grow because it is why we are here." There is great deal of wisdom when you say, it is claustrophobic and do not think about the fear of the unknown, think about the joy of it. In your experience, whether it was when you were being raised or something you saw in your mom's experience, when did you know you had fearlessness?*

K: At the age of nine and ten I went to Catholic school and I had to go to confession. I wouldn't be able to sleep the night before because I didn't have anything to say. What do I say? I don't want to lie. What sin can a kid of nine or ten have to confess? What did I do? I grew up in a household where the belief in God was very heavy. I always believed in God, however, I did start asking myself, why? What is the purpose of life? I was a 10-year-old trying to figure out the purpose of life and I couldn't figure it out. I think that's when I started to become a little fearless. That's also when I started dancing.

I forced myself out of my comfort zone to be a more rounded person. I was very shy as a child. So, I told my mother, I wanted to dance because I knew if I could dance in a room full of people, I could do anything. I slowly started setting goals to open up my personality. Through each step I became more fearless. Now my attitude is, what's fear? I don't know what it is. Actually, I do sometimes, but it doesn't control me.

A: *Fear doesn't stop us. Let's explore this a little deeper.*

There are a lot of children who take ballet, dance, sports, or musical lessons because parents or someone told them to. However, as a child you said wanted to dance to overcome something. This is rare in an adult, let alone a child.

Let's go back to the to the business. What kind of obstacles did you have to overcome when you were starting your business?

K: I started with $500.

A: *You used a $500.00 tax return check to start up your business.*

K: I purchased a printer and some ink. I made brochures and I used the rest of the money for my first month's rent, which was $350.00

People were saying, "How are you going to start a business with no clients?" I felt, if I build it, they will come. I didn't let having no clients stop me from my goal. Getting started was fairly easy, I think one of the biggest obstacles I had to face was the space. I was sharing it with a real estate agent and at the end of my lease, he told me he wasn't going to renew because I was using the space too much. I was actually developing clientele. I guess he thought, "Oh, here's this young girl with a crazy idea. Let me have her move in so we can split the rent." But when it actually started becoming a business and he told me I had to leave, this was the biggest problem I had to face. Where am I going to go because I'm new to this whole thing? I went on Craigslist and found a space. It was a little bit bigger. It was a little nicer.

Two years ago, our main location caught on fire and was closed for nine months. We were located in the basement of a church and when I say basement, I mean moldy pipes, big radiators, which sang, and still our clients came. We kept attracting new clientele and it gave me a lot of confidence.

When you overcome a certain number of things, you know you have to hold on tight because things always occur, you hold on until something good happens.

A: *Are you someone who prepares or someone who wings it?*

K: I've taught myself how to prepare, but I definitely started out winging it. It didn't hurt me. I feel people prepare too much, and don't take the first step. I'll take the first, second, third, fourth step and then I'll start planning. I think it has helped me get to where I am, not being afraid to take the first step.

A: *Let's just go back over something because there are powerful areas you talked about. Do not over prepare, however, some leaders will say the opposite. They tell people to, "Build business plans in great detail. Have a mission and vision statement, then start." I agree you need a base plan, but you can over prepare, as*

159

you said. Control your time. The fear of the unknown can prevent you from a joyful life. When it's over for you, what do you want your legacy to say?

K: Honestly, when my main location was lost in a fire, I realized my business was about way more than me. We were standing outside the building, the flames exploding and this guy beside me says, "I just bought a ten pack of stretching sessions." He didn't know I was the owner and he's worried about his ten-pack investment. At that moment, I realized it's not about me anymore. It's about helping everyone else, the employees and the clients. My whole intent is to be an example of breaking the mold and helping others to set their own personal goals, to know what their lives can look like, feel like, and not to be afraid to keep going. When people see my story, I hope they will find the confidence to believe in themselves.

A: *We spend our lifetimes just trying to get to this very answer. Let's talk about models for a second. You are a young entrepreneur. You were named one of the top female entrepreneurs this year by Huffington Post. Congratulations, quite an achievement. What are some stereotypes you have experienced?*

K: First of all my age, that's why sometimes I wear lipstick, to add at least five years.

A: *I try not to be shocked during a podcast, but I have to tell you, I was not prepared for that answer. So it adds five years?*

K: Yes, that's number one. I can walk into a room full of people, most of the people in the franchising world are at least fifty-five and over, and they think, "Who is this?" I have to go into that room and say, "I'm a serious business person." It's like proving myself.

Then there is being a woman. Sometimes I've been in situations where I haven't been taken seriously, until I start ripping through my accolades about what I've done, and then the respect is given to me. Just walking into the room, it doesn't happen, especially in the traditional corporate world.

Then being a minority. I've been told "Wow, you're an exception" or "There's not many of you." They beat around the bush trying to say, it must have been hard for me to get here because I'm a minority.

A: *It's fascinating because I do not think people understand the dynamics involved, whether it's intended to hurt or not, they are really saying, "Wow, it's surprising because there are not many smart, driven, entrepreneurial, black women." As a CEO, a sixty-four-year-old white man, I can state what you were perhaps being careful to avoid saying.*

K: A sixty-four-year-old man with amazing eyebrows.

A: *Oh, no, it's going be very hard to keep focused with you. Thing is, I can say it because I see it, even with my own colleagues. At Marsh & McLennan Northeast, eighty-five percent of my senior leadership team, and throughout my organization, are women. Over the last three years, seventy-eight percent of our new colleagues are minorities. People ask me, "How did you do it?" We just looked for candidates who did not look like me.*

We have been blessed with good performance, and to my colleague's credit, we attract great talent. Now, I truly believe our success is due to our diversity.

Did you begin to attract more diversity of thought around you as you became successful? Listeners love to hear from someone like you because you're unusual. You speak to our younger listeners. What happened to the crowd around you? How did it change as you became more successful?

K: How do I even begin?

When I first opened my storefront in Montclair, most of the business owners and my associates were older baby boomers. Then here's me, this millennial with a business idea, and they were the people around me. Then, I slowly started to attract more people my age who saw what I was doing and started to inquire and ask "How did you do this?" "How did you do that?" Then I realized, I think they're starting to see ways for them to do the things they want to do because they see me doing it. Now my crowd is my age, the people who contact me for strategic partnerships, they're younger, where before they were much older.

A: *What a success story. Think about what you just said, you're helping an entire generation get there quicker because of what you did. What a wonderful legacy. It's the same, in your world or my world. When I walk into a room, all people want to know is, why spend time with you? There is often a bias, the truth is people are judging you. They are determining if you have it together, if they are going to take a risk on you and if they believe you have built the correct foundation. You are helping a lot of people by being you.*

K: Most of the people who are reaching out to me through traditional franchise sources have been people who are retiring and are looking for ways to invest their money. They're already well off. This is just another avenue for them. They are thinking, "Who can I place in there to run it for me?" That's why you see a lot of franchises with management and the owners are off doing whatever they want. I noticed it and asked myself, "How can I help people?" There's such a divide in the franchise world. You have to have resources to just fill out the application.

I want to use all of this great knowledge I've gained to help people who aren't traditional franchisees. It is my strategy; helping people who would never be able to own anything.

A: *How wonderful. You are right, there are lots of franchises out there you would love to be a part of, but the buy-in is too great or the procedure is too difficult. With the high buy-in amounts, the legal components and all of the compliance pieces, the average person struggles to get a foot in the door.*

Let's go back to you as a ten-year-old. What was it like for you? Did you have freedom of thought? Was it encouraging? I want you to speak to the young parents, to help them create an environment for success. What would you say?

K: My father died when I was eight, he had an asthma attack and died. So early on, I realized I wasn't going to have someone whom everyone else may have. It was kind of challenging, but my mother was very supportive of any dreams I had. She used to tell me, "You don't have a boss. God is your only boss" She wasn't super religious, she was only saying don't call anyone boss. I used to think she was crazy. I clearly have a boss. But then when I started working in different environments, I would look at my quote-unquote "Boss" and think, "Why do I have to play the role of employee?" It's fine to be an employee obviously, but why do I have to say, "Okay this is where my life stops." I started asking myself these questions because I grew up with a mother who never put a limit on my capabilities. I almost blame her for my non-stop goal setting. I have an eight-year-old son and my intent is to be able to care for him, but also be involved with his life and not have to work twenty-four-seven. I would say, you can live your dreams and provide for your family at the same time.

If you're unhappy, you have to find ways to live a happy life because life is too short. You don't want to look back and ask yourself, how happy were you with a boss? I had a boss who used to motivate me, encourage me, and then she died. She was thirty-nine and died because she was completely stressed out at work. Her heart just stopped. She worked all the time and after she passed, I started to see things differently.

A: *I want to break the statement down a little bit because you said your mom said, "No one is your boss." Here at Marsh & McLennan Northeast, we have a culture where everyone is a CEO. Yes, you have an employee ID number, but there is nothing you do in a day which should prevent you from being amazing, having your own thoughts, and acting like an owner. It doesn't matter if there are hundreds of us, we're all better because we are all the CEOs of our lives. Why do people still struggle to achieve?*

K: They all have potential. It's fear. I've asked several people, "What's stopping you?" And they've all said, "Fear." Fear of failure.

You have to ask yourself, "What happens after failure?" Do you die? Do you crumble up into dust? I won't make any money? And - What if you do?

The biggest challenge is to encourage people and to breathe life into them. I think people are so busy nowadays, they don't believe things will actually work out, they dismiss it because they assume it won't work.

A: *What is amazing is you did not talk about the financials, about money. Financially you're very successful. I know you've done well financially, but it's not about money for you.*

Many people are focused on the money. They think success is driven by the financial part; money is their motivator. You don't think that way, do you?

K: Not at all. I grew up in poverty, basically.

A: *Define poverty for you.*

K: After my father died, my mother had to support my brother and me. We didn't have a car. We only could go grocery shopping when she got a check from work, so the food had to last. One of our greatest memories was going grocery shopping. We had to carry the bags seven blocks and when we got back, we were able to eat whatever we wanted. Having to ration your food, not being able to afford a real bed; my mattress was on the floor. I never had a bad childhood, but I definitely had secondhand clothes. I couldn't do certain things. I couldn't get the twenty-five-cent gum ball from the supermarket. Now, I'm like, Mom, do you want some gum balls?

I experienced my father's death at an early age, so I started to seek more from life, real heartfelt things and money is just the tool being used to provide for others.

One of my friends asked me to make a list of what my ideal life looks like, house, car, how much does that cost? You realize you don't need millions of dollars in order to live a happy life. What do you do with the extra money?

Do you employ people? Do you allow them to feed their families? For me, especially in the franchise world, where it is all about, "Did you sell a franchise yet?" I'd rather find a good candidate. I'm not going to accept money because it grows my income.

A: You grow very thoughtfully with your type of model and system. You could be opening far more locations, but you don't, you stay very thoughtful. Four, five, not twenty, not twenty-five, because you are all about the quality of your studios.

Let's go back to something we were talking about earlier when we talked about the crowd around you. You did this on your own. People were supportive. You had clients, and people show up, but what is the fabric inside you? What will always sustain you? How do you know, no matter what you do, you will be OK?

K: I could have been defeated mentally and financially. I could have gone bankrupt. I was starting my business with five hundred dollars, not knowing anything about capital or needing three months in reserve. I've gone through all the obstacles and I'm still here. Being able to be here with you, I know deep down inside, my mission is much greater than anything I could have ever imagined. I still don't know exactly what it is, other than helping and inspiring people. Deep down inside, I know I have a purpose.

We all get stressed out. For example, one of our employees, one of our coaches, a great kid, twenty years old, was kicked out of his house this morning and his family lives out of state, so he's homeless. This morning we're looking at different resources in the area to see how we can help him. He's still at the studio working. This is what propels me to keep going and to keep helping because I don't give up. I feel like if I give up, I'll give up on a lot of people other than myself.

A: *I'm very blessed to have you in the studio today, Kika thank you for sharing your story. You are an amazing woman and you've achieved what many in their heart want to, but in their mind are afraid to do.*

There are companies with mission statements on a brochure and a website or social media, but the people do not embody it. You are an entrepreneur and a businesswoman in a business with a mission of its own, which is powerful and unusual.

When you hear the name Kika Stretch Studios in the future, it's not just the name of business, it is a movement, a powerful movement started by a woman to help people on their paths to greatness.

Anything before we end the show?

K: Oh, how do I follow that up? First of all, thank you so much. This is what I want to do; have the platform to inspire others.
Keep listening to the show it's amazing. Don't give up. If you ask

yourself, "Should I give up?" What reason do you have to give up other than fear? So just try facing fear and see what happens. It's like building a muscle, after a while, you'll realize you're stronger. If there's one thing I could say to everyone, it is don't give up, try one more time. Don't give up and see what happens.

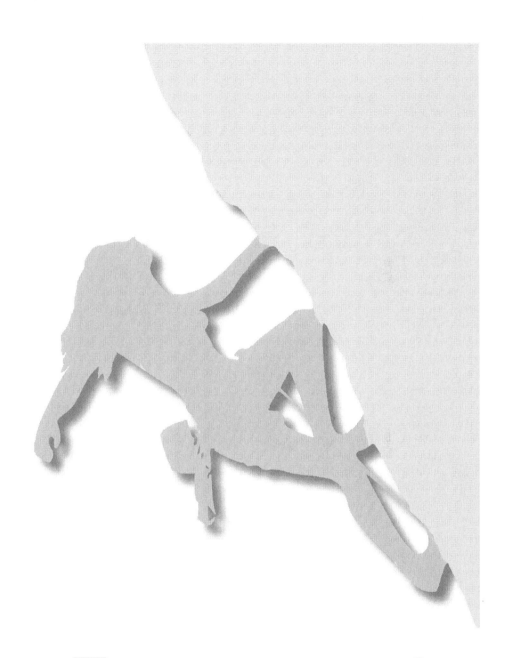

Excuses and
Objections

You took the challenge & stepped into the light of Leadership. Your example serves to inspire others to leave the darkness of doubt & succeed. You define motivation.

We don't all start with the same opportunities in life. Some are born into families who give them the best education, healthy food, great connections, and every resource they could ever want. Others are born into poverty where they do not receive an adequate education, receive poor nutrition, and virtually no connections to help them find success in life. Still, others have a decent start, but tragedy strikes repeatedly. No matter what they do, life seems to keep ripping the rug out from under them, leaving them beat up and defeated. Our start is only the beginning of our story, it isn't the most important part. There will be many times along our journey when our choices will steer our ship in different directions toward the conclusion of our bioepics. What happens between the beginning and the end is dependent on us.

What Hakika Dubose-Wise Taught Us

People told Hakika Dubose-Wise franchising was too hard for her to bother doing, and yet, she chose to Push the Possible to become the youngest woman franchisor.

Her father died when she was eight-years-old and she was raised by her entrepreneurial single mother who struggled to put food on the table. Even though she grew up poor, she found a way to go to a University and study dance, however after graduating she discovered she did not enjoy working in the entertainment industry. Kika didn't dwell on the tradegy she pursued triumph.

It wasn't easy and nay-sayers voiced their opinions on why she wouldn't succeed; she is young, a woman, and a minority in America. She Pushed her Possible by not allowing other people's judgments to interfere with her goals.

She did not let anything stop her from succeeding, not when her first landlord refused to renew her lease or when her main location burnt to the ground. Today, she continues to step into uncomfortable situations to prove herself, to Push for the Possible and to grow her dream bigger than she ever imagined.

Your mind and body work together to bend around challenge and bridge any barrier

Dream Chasing

Everyone has a dream, however, few excel beyond the average to Push the Possible, to shine, and to realize their dreams. I want you to move beyond the dreaming part and start Pushing your Possible to bring your dreams into the world of reality.

What does it take to make a dream reality? Hard work and passion.

You have to discover what doesn't occur to others in your industry, what they refuse to do, or are too lazy to do. You cannot look for the easy road. You must be willing to sacrifice, struggle, and stumble, like those whom I interview on the Roots of Leadership Podcast. They all decided to take the necessary steps to build the life they wanted. Will you?

When I started in the Insurance industry, my dream was to make a difference in the world of behavioral science. I knew what it was like to support kids who had it tough in residential care, and I wanted to do what I could to help them. To do this, I needed to learn everything I could about the industry by making connections, learning, and showing up to do things that did not occur to my competitors. I got into the facilities, visited clinics, and I asked questions of anyone willing to talk to me about their day-to-day operations. It took months for me to learn everything I needed to in order to help the people I wanted to help. AND...I didn't get paid to show up. No one of influence saw what I was doing and I didn't go around telling people about it. I was quietly helping, volunteering, and learning. My purpose was to discover their needs and figure out how to make their lives better with the products and services I had available.

Dreams are wonderful, but without hard work, they remain non-materialized potential, however, if you want them to become a reality, you need to get your head out of the clouds, get on the street, and do the work. I hear people say, "Someday I'll start," and someday is always tomorrow. Their dreams never become a reality because they don't want to do the hard work. The work they don't get paid to do, the stuff no one sees them doing, which may or may not result in revenue. They want to get paid, get a pat on the back, be given a promotion, and all with as little effort as possible.

Ask yourself, are you working to the best of your ability, doing everything possible to live your dream, or are you too busy just planning? Your dream is not on social media and it is not going to be handed to you. You need to get out there, make connections, and work harder than anyone else.

Obstacles

When you chose to execute your dream, to place each brick in its place, you will come face to face with destructive things called obstacles whose sole purpose is to stop you from placing the next brick or destroying the wall you just finished, and steering you off course through doubt, distraction, and discomfort. There is no journey to success without obstacles. They exist to teach you lessons, how to pivot, make you stronger, and show you the way to success.

I think a large obstacle people have is being afraid of what other people will think of them. They have heard people criticize each other, point fingers, and cast judgments their whole lives and do

174

not want to be ostracized, talked about, or judged. People judge, whether you chase your dream or not, so you might as well reach for the brass ring.

You are passionate, you have potential and you can perform, however the minute you start worrying about what others will think, you are at a deep disadvantage. The reality is, others do not have a vested interest in what you are doing, so they do not care enough to have a well thought out, honest, and valuable opinion.

There will also be times when the people who love you will try to stop you because they are scared for their security, fear for their dreams, and possess a limited vision. The thing is, they don't mean what they say because they haven't thought it through and may not understand what you are trying to accomplish.

Your partner or spouse will need to believe in you and your dream, especially if they are asked to sacrifice their time with you, take on more responsibility for the family, or are expected to roll up their sleeves to help you.

Be honest with your family. Tell them what you are planning, predict your success, and let them know you must work long hours, travel more, miss birthdays or recitals. Acknowledge their fears, concerns, and needs when you explain why you are working as hard as you do. If you are going to build a business, a great career and a successful life, you will need to make the hard choices and it will take sacrifice. By clearly communicating with those whom rely on you, they will want to help and work with you because they are part of the solution, the journey, and your success.

Not everyone has a supportive life partner or spouse. No matter how well you communicate your dream, they will not believe in it. They have their own reasons for standing in the way of your dream and in these cases, you will have to ask hard questions to find out why they do not want to back you.

Are they scared you will lose the house, their social-economic status or the children's education fund? Are they overburdened by the household chores already and can't see themselves taking on more of the family responsibilities?

Do they have a dream they feel will be sacrificed as a result of yours being fulfilled? Have you disappointed them one too many times by dreaming and not doing the hard work to succeed? Do you constantly break promises and only focus on your goals?

Be honest with yourself. Only you know the truth.

If the people in your life are not supportive, negative, or create obstacles for you, remove them from your support system. They can still be a part of your life, just not a part of your professional life. I'm not saying you have to divorce an unsupportive spouse but it is important your partner is on the same page as you. I'm referring to unsupportive friends, parents, in-laws, coworkers, neighbors, or extended family.

What are you willing to do, which no one will see, to leave the world a better place than you found it?

Networking is an invitation for strangers to connect. Networking opportunities usually have a warm energy about them because even shy people want to be approached and included. The genuine networker is the gatekeeper for everyone to begin a journey of opportunity. I encourage you to seek out five networking opportunities per month. Go there alone, set as a goal to meet ten people per event. From those ten find two prospects.

Excuses

When people make excuses for their lack of success, it limits them from achieving their true potential. Those who say, "Well, I didn't have the same opportunity somebody else did." believe they can only aspire one step above where they came from. They limit themselves by coming up with reasons why they cannot reach higher and must stay in their comfort zone.

Some use their past success as an excuse to stay where they are especially if they already accomplished more than their parents did. "I was the first to graduate from college in my family. I was the first to own a business. I was the first to travel." Great, congratulations on your achievement. What is the goal for tomorrow? Celebrate your achievement and then reach for the next one.

People on social media will reach out to me saying, "You don't know what I had to live with. You don't know what I struggled with." They are right, I don't know, but they can either move beyond it or they let the past define them.

If you can abandon excuse making, you can become someone

who can coach themselves and others, who can be entrepreneurial in your thinking, and consistently learn to think like and owner. Moving beyond circumstances of birth, traumas or the critical actions and words of others, you can coach others to be successful too. You can then move beyond traditional thinking by letting go of the victim mentality to realize your real potential.

The key is to not make limiting assumptions about your abilities and potential based on messages you receive from others around you.

When dealing with others' expectations, we are often faced with issues forcing us out of our game plan. The expectations of others, whether high or low, force us to abandon our vision, motivation and our personal dynamic marketing plan. Stay true to your instincts whether it is keeping a realistic perspective, learning from your failures, or collaborating with your personal advisors.

What else can you achieve? Your life is far from over, there is so much more you can do with it. You are not done. Even when you retire, you can still learn something new, travel to places you have never seen, and volunteer to help make the world a better place than you found it.

If you aren't dead, you have a purpose, you can contribute, and you are valuable to society if you keep moving forward.

Objections

Often times we run into objections which inhibit our success. Whether we are trying to sell a product, service, or ourselves we can come up against clients or people who will throw an objection in front of us. By understanding what the objections are, what the true need is, and being honest about what you have to offer, you will be able to manage any objection.

In my career I have heard every objection imaginable, from why someone didn't want to sign a deal, to killing a strategic plan I had proposed, and still I succeeded because I learned to dissect and understand the objections, therefore putting the needs of my clients or company before my own agenda. I am a consultative resource, not a transactional and this approach has served me well.

The saying, "Objections are not really nos," means we simply did not meet the needs of the person we were offering our service to, which is a basic explanation of all the marketing and sales books I have ever read about on how to handle objections. There is a foundation for handling objections, which I think will minimize the rejection process for you in the future.

Do not be afraid to immediately react to the objection. I believe one of the best things you can do at the end of a meeting is ask the participants how they honestly felt the meeting went. If you sense there is a lack of trust on their part, before the meeting ends, address the murky and cloudy issues. It is important to understand the objection to be sure you can adequately build a response.

Listen to the objection. Don't take it personally. Objections are healthy and they're critical to the decision-making process. It is much worse if the prospect stays stay silent. Then unpack the objections and reapproach with a newly tailored solution.

Question the Objection. People frequently use standard objections. It is an easy way to create a smoke screen to protect them from having to go deeper into the discussion or address a roadblock that hides the true objections. For example, it is simple to say, "Your price is too high or I wanted the red one." Question the objection; you will be respected for it, and in fact, your prospect or client will be encouraged by the process and you will uncover their real need.

Qualify the Objection. People do not put equal weight to all objections. Some are minimal and others are major. People verbalize objections as they think of them but not in the order of importance. It is up to us to place objections into a pattern or grid to help to identify the important objections to aid in the decision-making process. Win-win solutions are the result.

Capitalize and Close on the Objection. We can all learn a great deal from the way we handle objections. It helps us build our strengths and minimize our weaknesses. Most importantly, we have to capitalize on the objections by learning from them and addressing them to the best of our ability and then close on the issue. If you cannot solve the objection, it is important to honestly communicate this to the client and offer resources for them to find what they need.

Concede. There are some objections on which we need to concede, No Means No. No matter what we do in our marketing plan or delivery system we still may have to concede an objection to the individual if they truly do not need our service or product. We must respect the person's best interest over our interest. This is very healthy as it brings integrity and honesty into the process.

Decision Time. Once you have handled all the objections someone has proposed, it is important to ask for the decision. Whether the decision is favorable or unfavorable, at least it is closed, and you can move on. Files are littered with dead proposals of marketers and professionals who were unsuccessful because they may have handled the objection, but they could never ask for the close.

As individuals we must bring closure to everything we do. If you reflect back on your life to the experiences you did not successfully close and put behind you, are they the ones which still follow and haunt you today? The reality is, if you don't learn how to make closure part of your personal dynamic marketing plan and part of your personal delivery system, then your career and your personal life will always be filled with open-ended issues.

Push Your Possible

Excuses and Objections

This is the part of the book where you dive deeply into the concepts to form your own opinions, make plans, and set goals.

I encourage you to mark up the pages and make this book a resource for your life journey.

Want to share your thoughts with me on social media? Tag me in your Twitter or LinkedIn post and use the hashtag, #PushersofPossible.

Obstacles & Excuses

Make a list of obstacles and excuses that got in your way in the past. List how the excuses hindered your success or put you on a different path.

Skills & Knowledge

Make a list of the skills you have and the topics you are an expert in. What do you bring to the table today?

Skills & Knowledge

Make a list of the skills, resources, and knowledge you need to make your dream come true.

Skills & Knowledge

How can you obtain the skills, resources, and knowledge you need to make your dream a reality?

The obstacle: _____

Things you have NOW to overcome the obstacle:

Things you need to have to overcome the obstacle:

Where can you get the things you need?

Avoid looking over your shoulder, you may miss the turn to your next opportunity

Roots of Leadership
Steve Maneri

Listening to Steve Maneri's podcast, you would think you were listening to Monday Night Football. After all, where else would you expect to hear a former NFL tight end explaining how he mentally prepares to win a game? As it turns out, Maneri fits perfectly as a guest on The Roots of Leadership. Whether he is strapping on a football helmet at the stadium or adjusting his Windsor Knot tie in front of a mirror, Maneri knows that success comes from following a disciplined playbook.

Anthony takes a special interest in the non-profit, The Kids Dream Big Foundation, which Steve founded. The foundation mentors kids and teaches them about how to build a successful mindset through sports. Halfway through the episode, Maneri also shares some special advice he picked up from current New England Patriots Quarterback, Tom Brady.

189

The Interview

A: *This is Anthony Gruppo, and welcome to today's episode of the Roots of Leadership. I'm here today with Steve Maneri, a leader and an overachiever. He is a former NFL tight end offensive lineman. He was a standout at Temple University and is currently with Colliers International in Corporate Real Estate. Steve played in the NFL for ten years with the New England Patriots, the Kansas City Chiefs, the Chicago Bears, and the New York Jets, but it doesn't stop there. Besides being a leader of tremendous record, he also formed The Kids Dream Big Foundation. I'm honored to have Steve here today, welcome to the Roots of Leadership Podcast.*

S: Anthony, it's great to be here. Thank you for having me.

A: *Steve, I think many have the dream of being a professional athlete. How did it start for you?*

S: It was when I was a senior in high school, right before the season, I went to Brookdale Park, and ran a forty-yard dash. I said, if I run under four-nine, I'm going to play football this year. I thought if I ran fast enough, there might be a future for me in football. I ran it in under four-nine seconds according to a friend of mine, so, I decided to join the football team. That was August of 2006.

A: *It was just you and a friend in a field with a stopwatch. Is that how you lead your life? You set some kind of objective or goal and then test yourself against it?*

S: Yes, that's exactly how I've approached my successes. I went out there and said, "I'm going to play football and see where it takes me." I ended up getting a lot of attention from college coaches and before I knew it, I was playing at Temple University.

A: *When you were at Temple, you also excelled academically, how did you balance the intensity of sport with the rigors of academics?*

S: I think the way you do anything, step-by-step, not looking at the big picture, because if you look at the big picture you wake up on Monday morning and say to yourself, from seven am to nine pm, I'm going to be busy. I'm going to have no time to rest, no time to do this, do that, and you get overwhelmed. I look for little parts of the day and achieve them. Once I get that done, I take the next step and that's how I became the player I was. That's how I'm becoming the broker I am. Achieve successes in small increments.

A: *A lot changed for you Steve. In just two years you went from being undrafted in 2010, to one of the highest-ranked blocking tight ends in 2012. What happened to Steve Maneri in those 24 months?*

S: Interestingly enough, I was a tight end in college. In my first two years in the pros, I was a tackle. Tackles are guys who can't run and can block. They wanted me to play offensive lineman, so I gained 30 pounds in a year to be a tackle. Then they switched me back to tight end, which is the year you're talking about. With the mentality of an offensive lineman, I went out there every day knowing I wasn't beating anybody by running routines and getting open. I made the point of every play to block someone, to finish them, and make highlights. It really paid off for me that year.

A: *You had to change jobs time and time again, same career, new city, new coach, a new model of running a system mentally. How did you prepare?*

S: It's all about perspective. I think you can look at my situation in two different ways. You can say, I played on six teams in six years and was released from all those teams, or you can look at it as, I was undrafted and had to fight and claw my way to successful seasons, which is probably a group of less than 1%.

A: *Besides perspective, was there an on-off switch for you because when I met you, I saw a professional guy who certainly has a boardroom presence. Yet, you have this constant look of intensity. Who is Steve Maneri?*

S: I always want to be a winner at everything I do. It is a longer process in the corporate world. I'm thirty years old with less than three years in the corporate environment; it's a process I'm still learning. Football has a faster gratification, where you work all day, all week from Monday to Saturday and then Sunday comes and you either win or lose, it's almost instant weekly gratification. In the corporate world, it's a little different. I am someone who's trying to achieve all those little tasks every day to become someone as successful as you, for example.

A: *Thank you for that. Even at sixty-four, I feel like every day I'm learning something new. Let's talk about doing the little things. Why do people struggle with focus and discipline to stay at it? You had to stay at it for all of your career. I see professionals struggle with peaks and valleys, and I ask myself, Why? What's your perspective?*

S: People get blinded by the outcome. My college coach, Alec Golden, was a great mentor, a great person, he always said, "Trust the process and love the process."

When I said it is about the little things, achieving the little goals, I was thinking about when I was a rookie with the Patriots in 2010. One day, I sat next to Tom Brady in the lunchroom. In 2001 he was a rookie, he was a sixth-round pick, he wasn't a starter. He was a third-string quarterback, nine years later, he's Tom Brady star quarterback. It was just me and him at the table. He was eating his lunch and I was sitting a couple of seats over, more than a little nervous to talk to him. Finally, I got up the courage to ask, "How did you know then that you were going to be great? Did you know you were going to be Tom Brady?" He said, "No, I was just trying to make the team, I just wanted to make the team." It really hit home for me.

A: *When you said, 'Trust the process,' here at Marsh & McLennan Northeast, we have a model called the Six Degrees model. When we train people, we explain this is the model, our playbook. You can put your own style inside it, but you are going to run the plays, you are going to run the model.*

Successful organizations and leaders have a process which people can learn and follow. I would say to all the leaders out there listening, if you have a process, stick with it, help people learn it. Don't constantly change it. If you tinker with the plan too much people cannot learn it. Would you agree?

S: I do. The perfect example is when I was with the Patriots. As soon as someone steps out of line, I don't care how good you are, you were gone. I was there in 2010 when Randy Moss got released for speaking up a little too much. If you did not trust the process and follow the guidelines, you were at risk of losing your job, or not being successful anymore. The process was proven to work over and over again, so you were expected to follow it.

A: *Here it is not a community control environment. I encourage people to speak up because their ideas may be valid and we can improve. However, if you're speaking up just because you don't want to run the drill, engage in the process of the practice, and just be a distraction, someone is going to cut you.*

In the world of sport, you had an advantage others may not have because you had to work hard in a very competitive environment. What did you learn? Somebody wanted your job every day and if an injury happened you were at risk. How did you mentally adjust?

S: Well, you said it. The NFL is competitive so I needed to make sure I was doing everything I possibly could, every day. There were hundreds of guys killing themselves to get better and take my spot. The second you get complacent is the second you lose your job. It's happened many times in professional sports, not just football, but all the sports. How do I mentally prepare myself? It's partly fear-based. The fear of investing, the fear of failure, the fear of losing your job, and knowing there's a guy knocking on the door who is probably more athletic than me.

A: *I have a definition of fear in my first book, 'Creating Reality Guide to Personal Accomplishment.' Fear is a total of lost moments. Do you have a detailed practice schedule in business as you had as a player?*

S: No, I mean, as a player, you're regimented. In my business, it is wide open. There are a lot of different ways to be successful in the commercial brokerage business. I don't have a plan. I'm on a great team and I learn from everyone around me. My mantra, in the beginning, is to learn as much as I can from people around me because what everyone does in any great business is to follow the greats. You follow the successful people. That is how you learn. I think part of being a leader is your ability to follow.

A: *I think it's okay to challenge the people whom you pick as a role model or mentor because someone may have been in business for 20 years, and now they want to mentor someone else or coach them, however as a mentor, they may not bring their best game. They are not at the top of their own game. They are not lifetime learners and they are not challenging themselves. It doesn't matter how long I've been in business, I am still challenging myself to make improvements, because if we do not, if we stop being lifetime learners, we deserve to be passed by.*

S: I think you are a great example of that. I mean, you're sixty-four-years old and you're very active on social media. You followed the path of someone closer to my age to get to that level and you've been more successful in what you're doing. You're doing a great job. The ability to follow supports your ability to lead as the CEO of Marsh & McLennan Northeast.

A: *Thank you. I hope the younger professionals, who are comfortable with social media learn from me. If they see me try it and I slip or fall, it works or doesn't work, they are encouraged because they receive different ideas, and together we are even more powerful. I'll have leaders my age ask, "Why are you* *branding yourself on social media, are you crazy?" However, this strategy has led to countless opportunities.*

Let's talk a little bit about your foundation because I was so excited to hear about it. The Kid's Dream Big Foundation, how did it start?

S: There are four founders. In 2014, I was having dinner in downtown Chicago after a charity event with another NFL player, Tony Moeaki. We were discussing how we can tell a kid to do something that his parents have told him to do hundreds of times and he doesn't listen, but as soon as it comes from a professional athlete, the kid listens. We wanted to harness that unique platform to try to mentor kids, and give kids role models to guide them in the right direction. Every kid wants to be a football player, a basketball player, a famous athlete. Thing is, ninety-nine percent of the athletes retire to become a professional in a different industry. Our primary focus is to help kids achieve success through what they learn in sports because we all did and our goal is to empower kids.

A: *Fantastic, not only does it have a great mission, but you're also serving as a role model. People attach themselves to professional athletes because they inherently know how hard it is to do what you did. I have so much respect for you, Steve, not only for being a successful professional athlete but at 30 years old you have successfully reinvented yourself. When you were reinventing yourself, what were you worried about?*

S: I was one of the best in the world in the NFL, at the top of the sport and it is very tempting to get into coaching, broadcasting, anything football related because I'm an expert at it. I'm twenty-seven years old going into a business I don't know anything about.

I'm a rookie, I'm as green as they come. It was a challenge. I had to become a sponge and learn as much as I could.

Don't worry about making money. Don't worry about the end goal or the outcome. Worry about the process and doing the best you can every day and then eventually, you'll hit where you want to hit.

A: *You are accurate Steve, impatient people fail to grind their way to greatness. They look for a secret sauce. However, you have to grind to greatness. It is Tom Brady's story and it is your story. It is any of the great stories from the locker room or on the field. Was there a moment when you said the grind was not worth it?*

S: There were plenty of times, because of the high-pressure situation for a guy like me, who is battling every August for a roster spot, and is always on the brink of making it or not. It's 110 degrees in Kansas City in the middle of August, it's week four of camp, day 26 and you have a bad practice, missed a couple of blocks, or twisted your ankle. You come off the field and then you have to sit in a room with the rest of the team who watched you screw up. Sitting there with you are other tight ends who are not on the team and are trying out for your spot in a pressure situation. At that moment, you focus on the epitome of the grind, put your head down, and only control what you can control. In the end, you have to know you did your best, did everything you possibly could, and have no regrets if you get cut.

A: *Now there is a lesson of leadership. It is one of the profound moments. If we can have no regrets and we do the best we can we can move forward if we fail. Some people are hard on themselves and beat themselves up, play it out to their friends,* *and get stuck in self-pity. I think of the pressure people create for themselves and I wonder if it is a way to compensate for the feeling of inadequacy. They seem to believe they need to be perfect and never fail to be accepted or liked, and they are wrong. It is those who try, fail, and try again who are sought after by leadership.*

S: We are all average in certain aspects of life. My message to people is the same message I gave myself when I realized I wasn't getting open on the football field. Find your strength and excel at it. Everyone is good at something. You can be really good at video games and it becomes a career. Have you seen the news lately? It is amazing, people are on their couch making hundreds of thousand dollars. It's crazy.

A: *I read an article today about converting a business to a gamified environment so people can learn by playing a video game. You can learn more about insurance and risk by playing a game. I don't have enough time on the clock of my game to figure it out. It's amazing, but it goes to my point that anybody can be good at something and find their passion. Find what you want to do and accelerate it into a career for yourself.*

You know Steve, I'm really honored to have you on the show today. Looking down the road you are going to be the person whom people study as a role model. What do you want to be remembered for? Steve, what do you want your legacy to be?

S: I appreciate you saying people are going to remember me and that's exactly what I want. When we started our foundation, I want kids to come up to me when I'm sixty-seven years old and say, "Steve Maneri, thank you because without your help, without your guidance, I wouldn't have been where I am today." Life is a game of choices, one choice can make you a CEO, another choice can make you a garbage man. I'm not saying it's bad to be either, it is about choices. It is what we do with our foundation. What I do in life. If people want to get into the real estate business, I help them. Helping people to be successful is what inspires me. Of course, the money's good and you want to make money, but at the end of the day, you're not burying yourself with your money.

A: *You have upped the grind Steve, it's really been a pleasure having you on the show.*

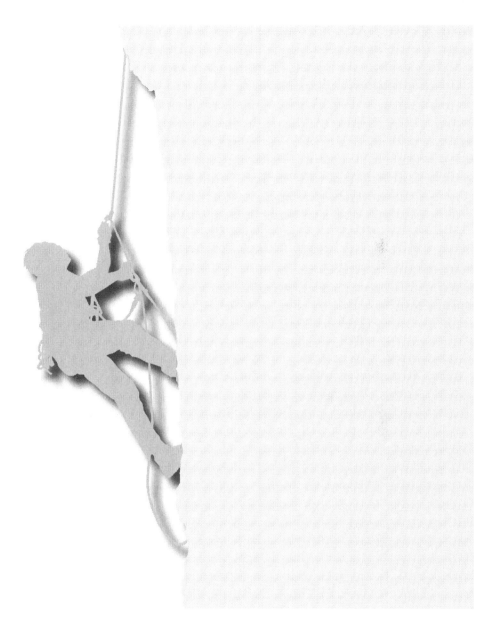

Routines and Strategy

Competition is a blessing and a curse, depending on how you use it.

Competition is a good thing when it is used to drive us to be better than a benchmark; be it a record, another person, or ourselves. Some people are naturally competitive and need to excel in everything they do, where others must search hard to find an ounce of competitiveness. As everything in life, too much of a good thing is a bad thing and not enough of a good thing is not good. A person can have too much or not enough competitive spirit.

Great leaders follow a daily routine to help them get everything accomplished and to ensure they live a full, well rounded life. Some people believe routines are confining, however, even these non-routine individuals have a routine. They get up, drink their coffee, get ready for the day, and go to work. Successful people go through their routine purposefully to ensure their goals will be realized and that they will be productive all day.

Professional athletes are both competitive and have strict routines to ensure they are improving their skills, staying fit, and getting better at their craft. Leaders in the business world do the same thing while wearing a suit.

What Steve Maneri Taught Us

Have a benchmark to test yourself against.

Take each day as it comes and focus only on what you have to do right now to effectively get to the next thing.

Put the effort in, even if you are not working within your specialty because you will learn important skills that will help you excel when you move into a position where you have more talent.

Have the right perspective when assessing your life, your work, and yourself. Look for the silver lining and the positive outlook of your life.

Trust the process. Work hard to improve your skills and stay competitive to keep your spot in the game.

Give back by mentoring others and inspiring younger people to learn through sport.

Fear is a complacency where if allowed to run unchecked, will start the domino effect of failure.

Always a Leader First

I never looked at being a successful insurance professional or a successful leader as two separate things. Everyone should see themselves as a leader first; a leader who happens to be in a certain job. I have never thought, "Great, I've hit a point where I'm successful," because success is always a moving target and is defined by the service you provide to humanity, not by the size of your bank account. There are two separate metrics by which to measure success to ensure you are on the right track. Ask yourself, do people come with me as I lead them into the Possible and if they follow, do they stick with me? If your life both personally and professionally is a revolving door of people, then the chances of your being successful are pretty slim.

This is a great way to judge your life, isn't it? If you are constantly having to seek out new friends, then you are unsuccessful at creating and maintaining relationships. The biggest indicator of success as a leader is the people whom you've helped along the way, in life and work. Revealing is the size of your network, how many people trust you or come to you for advice, and introductions they make to you of their own circle. People are the ones who bring you opportunities to grow and a force to drive you forward into the Possible, so if people aren't in your life, how do you expect to succeed?

I've never felt I was on the wrong path in life. I believe you are on the right road when you can still balance passion with happiness and performance, which I have always been able to do. With every job I have taken, I strived to be the best at it.

There are a lot of people who want to do something else as a career than what they are currently doing. Instead of becoming the best at what they currently do, they are always trying to become something different and then they are never satisfied. They are a ghost of themselves because they are not living up to their potential, or living with their passion. Make a contract with yourself where the terms and conditions are about your capabilities not your position. Your position then becomes a platform for your passion not merely a job and a paycheck.

It was popular in the sixties for people to take time to "find yourself." If someone didn't feel whole or comfortable in their own skin, didn't know who they were or where they wanted to go, or were without personal or professional direction, finding oneself was key. If they were not in control of their destiny, they allowed the wind to take them on a journey with no set course or outcome.

I've never lost myself. I have always known who I am, where I am, and what I want out of life. I may not have known the details, the hills, the valleys, or the rest stops, but I knew me, and I had a vision for my future. Believe that you fit everywhere and then you will feel you belong anywhere.

Positive Attitude

A positive attitude is the foundation for all positive outcomes because there are a lot of people who try to break you down and keep you from Pushing for the Possible. The definition of happiness and success is different for everyone. You have to find your own definition and then push toward it.

Attempt to create a truthful environment where you do not lie to yourself and those around you. Often times, if someone is fired, they will spin it saying, "I am now free to pursue something better because I wasn't appreciated there anyway." You are always free to pursue happiness, however, if you don't honestly reflect as to why you were fired and examine your own actions, you won't grow or improve. Debrief when negative or failure happens and learn from it.

I try to be very factual about what is happening because it helps me become more self-aware and honest with myself and others. During my career, I've been blessed to be asked to turn underperforming operations or individuals around. There have been times I had to succeed a leader who struggled and needed to be removed prior to my arrival. Often, they had created a negative culture where they were condescending, distant, or spoke at people, instead of with them. When I come in, I make it a point to meet the team, and thank them for doing a good job, which I am sincere about because they did do the best job they could in that environment.

Whenever I discover a success in my team's daily work, I give them a positive response and thank them for doing a good job. They quickly start to feel better about themselves and feel compelled to thank others, and before we know it, we have a community; not a culture. We foster a community where people are not so hard on themselves because they are afraid of losing something or being targeted by waves of negativity. When people work in a positive environment where they are supported, appreciated, and recognized for a job well done, they start to improve and excel. I then get the credit for turning an organization around, when all I did was authentically support people and empower them to look at themselves and others differently. The turn isn't in the financials, it's in the hearts and minds of the people who work there. When the mindset is right the desired outcome is achieved.

Simple.

Everyone strives to do the right thing and be successful. They want to serve others but when treated unfairly, they start to shine a negative light on others because they had the light of indifference shined upon them.

When I start working with people, I begin by trusting them, believing that they have my best interest at heart and that they have my back. I assume they don't want to see me fail and they don't want to fail. If I find the cynical nefarious outliers, I deal with them swiftly and directly. This approach works better than coming in and assuming everyone is out to see me fail, because they are not.

People want great leadership.

Open Door or Closed Door?

Though it is not as impactful or productive, it is easy to use the old adage, "It's lonely at the top."

Leaders must create beyond a healthy culture to evolve toward a collegial community where their people feel safe coming to them with anything. In order for people to thrive they need to be able to ask their leaders whatever they want, even if it is hard for them to say or for the leader to hear. Uncomfortable conversations are painful for everyone, however they lead to better ideas, closer relationships, and clarity of direction. Encourage people to come to you with professional problems, foster a safe environment by being approachable, take interest in their lives, and discuss small things with them.

Since leaders must have the difficult conversations, make the brutal decisions, and assign the arduous tasks, they have to walk a tight rope between being personable and being too personal. To do this effectively, they must keep a personal distance from those they lead while remaining friendly and engaged.

As a leader, I have to stay accessible but not allow myself to get too close personally to those whom I work with because I have to make complicated decisions every day, which will affect the lives of others. It is harder if the decisions I make will impact a friend. When a leader is detached from their team by not letting any one get close to them, hiding who they are, or being aloof, it keeps people guessing about what they are thinking and planning. How can a team be creative or trust in an environment where the leader is detached and mysterious? By engaging, showing your personality, and taking interest in your team's lives, you can provide access to yourself and keep a professional distance to enable you to make the decisions you have to make for the company.

I remember taking over an organization and walking around greeting people for the first time. I saw the shock on their faces. They were totally surprised because I had taken time to come and ask how they were doing, what they did in the company, and what they were working on. I received emails thanking me for saying, "Hello." It was a clear indication of the detached, inaccessible leadership style present before I got there. People should be allowed to interact with you in the workplace, as they can interact with you in life, because the decisions you make as an executive or leader impacts thousands of people and a leader should know whom he impacts.

Competitive Natures

You have to be more caring than competitive. Competitiveness helps you get through the struggles when people are trying to take your role or a position above you, however it can also cause you to take your eye off the ball.

There was an article about me in a UK publication, before I had even relocated, with statements made by unnamed sources of Marsh Commercial's competitors. They gave their opinions as to what I should think about and what might be difficult for me in the UK as compared to the USA. I found great humor in this because they were trying to distract me from my focus. They were afraid of what would happen when their competitor changed leadership. Whenever there is a change in an industry it causes uncertainty, disrupts the status quo, and makes people nervous. They became worried about what the new leader would do and the minute our competitors started to focus on what I should do, or what I might do, they were not focused on in-house operations, and the court advantage went to me.

They gave me the upper hand by being competitive. I can't help wonder what they are competing against. Their own insecurity? Uncertainty? Fear? Either way, advantage me.

Grinding

Grinding is when you keep working past the point of what you think is your limit. Grinding to greatness is doing the hard work in a consistent manner during inconsistent times. When faced with exhaustion, hurdles, or seemingly insurmountable challenges, those who don't appreciate the grind turn and run to greener pastures. Remaining on the original side of the fence and pushing through a hurdle will prove it is this side which holds the seed to far greener grass.

The following three tips will help you grind your way to greatness. Creativity can be found in sameness so use routine as a foundation to launch new ideas. Work in pairs instead of alone when the grind is tough. Know that when you are grinding it out, you are becoming stronger and learning to handle all forms of challenge.

If a person is driven by a win at all costs attitude, they will cut corners and do the wrong things at the expense of their team. However, if you have a drive to do the right thing at all costs, you can outlast the competition, no matter what they throw at you.

Personal Branding

The purpose of learning personal branding is for others to get to know your mission as you promote the mission of others. I have used multiple platforms to deliver my message to create new avenues of exposure and learning for a more successful outcome for myself and others. I built a broad foundation to house my brand. I currently have a website with a blog, a successful podcast, an engaged Twitter following, six published books, and strong connections on LinkedIn.

All of this coalesces to tell my brand story to the marketplace. It didn't happen overnight. In other words, it took experimenting, long hours, passion, drive, and lots of it. I am fortunate to have a team of talented people, like my producer Caryn and editor Kim, to help me. Over the course of a year we worked hard, created content to share on social media, and attracted an engaging audience.

By building an online following, I am able to help others find an audience for their brand. When I congratulated Jennifer Mosher, my successor at Marsh & McLennan Northeast, the message received thousands of views, and many of those followers went on to find out more about her. The news wouldn't have had the same impact if I'd posted it before I started building my digital personal brand.

I like being able to use my brand to bring exposure to others. It gives me great satisfaction when they see even broader success because I interviewed them or sent out a social media post about them. The podcast enables me to introduce new people to my amazing audience of loyal listeners, whom I love. Without my listeners, I wouldn't have the ability to provide a platform for leaders to share their stories and widen their brand's awareness.

If you are going to start a brand, think about who you are, what you want to say, and how you want to be perceived. You need to build your personal platform first, then use it to congratulate and highlight others. As it evolves over time, when you share stories, it will increase your brand even more. You will be seen as somebody altruistic, in the know, caring, respectful of others, and you not only concerned with yourself.

Why social media fails for some people is they are only talking about themselves and it can get boring. If you want to have success over the long-term, your audience needs to be entertained, educated, and engaged in your story. By introducing people to your audience, you are bringing added value and they will continue to follow you.

What is your purpose? Are you in 'it' for the followers or to add value to those who consume content online? There is enough shallow, boring, content out there. Find a purpose, a reason for people to follow you and if you consistently show up with good content, your following will grow.

Before Social Media, before blogs, before the internet, I was building my personal brand out in the real world. When I began, I booked speaking engagements, 'working-back-alleys', almost like an entertainer starts off, in a no name, small audience venue where they pay their dues and which eventually gets them to play the Vegas stage.

I spoke at high schools, grade schools, and libraries. Wherever I could to give back to the community and build a brand. In those days, we didn't think of it as building a personal brand, we called it marketing. It was what we did to build a reputation, spread our message, and become known for something, which today we define as being an influencer.

They Want Your Job

If no one's chasing what you're doing, then you are probably not doing it very well and not having any fun doing it. If you are Pushing your Possible you will leave your current position for the next exciting role in your journey. When you vacate your desk if you've done your job well, a member of your team will rise to take your place.

When I accepted my new assignment as CEO, of Marsh Commercial in the United Kingdom, the transition became a satisfying move vs. one of trepidation because my successor came from my leadership team. Each of the three candidates to replace me in New York were from my leadership team with no

Start your day with the thought of seeking to improve the day for others. You can make a difference by believing in yourself and others.

external candidates sought. When my successor was awarded the position, the other two candidates, even though they had the lens of disappointment to look through, were supportive of her, congratulated her, and felt blessed because the culture would continue as a community and ensure the transition would be as seamless as possible.

What a story of success for the team, for the community, for my legacy, and the transition to my successor. This is how it is supposed to work. A leader should mentor team members with the purpose of training them to take over when they move on.

Accountability

Develop a culture of the community based on human improvement, which allows for open accountability, not one based on a structure of bonuses and incentives. Corporate cultures using a ratings system will penalize those who make mistakes when they are trying to grow and reward those who are complacent and stay in their comfort zone. Performance ratings are based on a number, let's say one to five. Management believes no one can be a five because fives do not exist. Everyone with a three or better gets a bonus or salary increase. I believe complacency is where threes reside. If you have been doing the job long enough you should be a three because you know how to do the job. I'm more impressed by the individual who gets a two because they are trying to do something different, learn something new, and Push their Possible.

The person who is learning something new is bringing more value than the person who has done the job for 30 years always remaining a three. Now, I'm not saying that those people are not valuable, we need those consistent people who want to do the same job and do it well. They have real value to an organization like the chorus in a play. However, if you are going to develop people who are going to learn by doing new things and are willing to risk, you have to stop penalizing them when they make a mistake.

I'm not saying people can make the same mistakes over and over and be rewarded, that would be as absurd. People must learn from their mistakes and do their best to mitigate the risks to the company. One needs to be accountable to their team and the team's goals by asking for help and advice along the way. When a team is a community who supports one another, instead of competing with each other, everyone wins.

As a leader, I don't have to beat you, I have to achieve with you. I tell people, we must be accountable to each other. Start to value a person's work, not fear it and don't compete against it. Say to someone, "Thanks for doing this and let's work on it together because collectively I think we can better results and we will both improve." Do not say, "My God, my work is better than yours." You can either work to pass lower performing teammates and only get so far, or you can work together, and everybody can blow past the corporation's opponent.

Most of my career has been in a sales environment, which is competitive in nature. I was blessed to collaborate with people in the organizations, instead of against them. There are people from all over the world whom I can call because they do not see me as their competitor since I didn't do anything to harm their career. I may have surpassed them from a career standpoint due to overachieving, however, I didn't get here on my own. I succeeded because other people helped me to achieve my goals and I helped them to achieve theirs. What's wrong with people in a competitive environment working together as a team?

The Independent Professional

Some people don't work in a team environment, they work independently or are at the top of the corporate hierarchy. In these cases, a Personal Board of Directors will help an individual stay on track to meet their goals. Lone wolves should create a network of people to help talk them through challenges, perhaps a peer group of people who, like them, are in the same solo environment situation. There are plenty of people out there who need support and who are willing to offer it.

Some people cop out and say to me, "You don't understand Anthony, you have a massive Corporation behind you, an executive team. You have all of these tools and resources which I don't have to succeed. I don't have the support to stay on track the way you do." The thing is, some of the things that are there to help me, get in my way, whereas the solo performer isn't hindered by the personalities, decisions, corporate boards, shareholders and the needs of other people.

Everyone in the world has a talent, has a story, and a message. Telling your story will attract engaged followers to your platform. Ask yourself, what do you have to say? Why would the world listen? What talent can you showcase? Too many people stay quiet when they should talk, because we all have something to say.

Push Your Possible

Routine and Strategy

This is the part of the book where you dive deeply into the concepts to form your own opinions, make plans, and set goals.

I encourage you to mark up the pages and make this book a resource for your life journey.

Want to share your thoughts with me on social media? Tag me in your Twitter or LinkedIn post and use the hashtag, #PushersofPossible.

Daily Routine

Your morning routine

What does your morning routine look like NOW?

What do you want it to look like?

Daily Routine

Your evening routine

What does your evening routine look like NOW?

What do you want it to look like?

Daily Routine

Make a list of tasks you need to do every day to move toward your Possible.

Personal Brand

What do you want your reputation to say about you? Think about personality characteristics, professional traits, and what you want to be known for. Write your legacy story.

Personal Brand

Take an inventory of the platforms you currently have and determine which platforms you will need to broadcast your message on.

	Website		Pinterest Profile
	Blog		Reddit Profile
	Podcast		Quora Profile
	YouTube Channel		Other Social Media
	Webinars		Speaking Engagements
	Online Courses		Articles in the News
	LinkedIn Profile		Press Releases
	Twitter Profile		Media Kit
	Facebook Page		A Book

What types of content do you enjoy creating?

	Formal Articles		Twitter Posts
	Casual Blog Posts		Micro Blog Posts
	Case Studies		Graphic Quotes
	Research Papers		Webinars
	Vlog Videos		Video Courses
	Audio Podcasts		PDF Downloads
	Interview People		Booklets
	Photography		Other

Personal Brand

Take time to search the keywords Personal Branding on search engine's and social media. Make a list of "Experts" to follow and learn from.

*Wherever we stand
is our playground.
Whatever we dream
is our game.*

Roots of Leadership
Ainsley & Wolvie

As Jim Henson once said, "The most sophisticated people I know are all children". How can we tap into the childlike lessons of leadership? The ones which come so intuitively to us as kids, but we lose sight of as we enter adulthood? On today's podcast, we look back and explore those facets of leadership with our co-host and guest Ainsley, granddaughter of Anthony C. Gruppo.

Ainsley Jane is a kind, curious, and comical 10-year old. Through her love of Frozen and memories of building sandcastles with her "Wolvie," Ainsley's perspective is vital to understanding great leadership points with childlike wonder.

The Interview

Anthony: *This is Anthony Gruppo, and welcome to the Roots of Leadership. Today, my co-host is my granddaughter, Ainsley Karas. Ainsley, are you glad to be here with your Wolvie?*

Ainsley: Yes.

Anthony: *I'm so glad that you are here with me too. Wolvie is the name Ainsley calls me. Ainsley, where did we go last night?*

Ainsley: HP burger.

Anthony: *And what Broadway show did we see last night?*

Ainsley: Frozen

Anthony: *Yes, it was fantastic. What was your favorite part?*

Ainsley: When she made the icicles.

Anthony: *I know. I couldn't believe how wonderful that was. Well, I'm glad you're here as a co-host today. I asked Ainsley to join me to talk about the power of play and how important it is to keep our inner child active, excited, motivated and creative. Ainsley, the other night we were playing with your Lego set. What were we building?*

Ainsley: Pet Salon.

Anthony: *Yeah. You did a great job. It's so important to keep the child within us in active play. In leadership, and in our careers, we do daily tasks and life starts to take a hold of us and we begin to lose our creativity, which is sparked by our inner child. Ainsley, sometimes we are in a restaurant, what do we do with the sugar packets?*

Ainsley: Build a castle.

Anthony: *Yeah, sometimes we build castles and I don't know how other people look at us. The thing is, if you look at families dining out today, you often see the kids on their iPads, parents and teens on iPhones, and families aren't even engaged in a discussion. I wonder where the creativity of just building a castle with sugar packets at a table has gone? What happened to talking and playing with a child? It's more important to interact and connect with children than it is to play a video game.*

Ainsley, you are from Florida, is that right?

Ainsley: Yes.

Anthony: *Do you like to go to the beach?*

Ainsley: Yes.

Anthony: *What are some of your favorite things to do at the beach?*

Ainsley: Play, build castles.

Anthony: *Yeah, I like to build sandcastles with you. Sometimes life and business are a lot like building a sandcastle. It takes the right mixture of sand, water, and tools. If you think about business, think about life, sandcastles are important because when we build a castle, an opportunity, a system, or a model, sometimes it doesn't come out the way we envisioned it. Maybe the mold cracks, waves come up and the walls begin to crumble. Ainsley when you build sandcastle and they start to fall apart, what do you do?*

Ainsley: Make a moat

Anthony: *Making a moat is so important. Sometimes in life, we have to build a moat around the structure we're trying to build. It's not protectionism or isolation, it is putting a moat around our ideas and the problems we are trying to work on. It is using our inner child to be as creative as possible.*

I believe when we get to spend time with children, we think more creatively because they play with such a creative mindset. I love the time I get to spend with Ainsley, who is my oldest granddaughter. Cecilia is our youngest grand-daughter and at fifteen months old, we can already see her creativity.

Think about what you can do today, and in the future, to bring out your inner child. What were some of the games that you played as a child? What is the favorite thing you like to do with Wolvie, Ainsley?

Ainsley: Superheroes

Anthony: *Oh yeah. Who are the stronger superheros, the boy superheroes or the girl superheroes?*

Ainsley: The boys.

Anthony: *The boys! I'm surprised because you never let the boys win, it's always the super girls who win. Who are your superhero girlfriends? What are their names?*

Ainsley: Wonder Woman. Supergirl and Batgirl.

Anthony: *It's so much fun to play superheroes with you. We've even used Uncle Anthony's old Justice League castle. Are there villains when we're playing superheroes?*

Ainsley: Yes. They try to put bombs in front of the castle.

Anthony: *When Ainsley and I were talking about building castles in our careers or our lives, we were talking about how those castles collapse and you have to build a moat to protect them from the waves. Sometimes villains show up to blow up our castle and a moat won't protect it. In life we face opponents who blow up our castle and when that happens, it's our childlike creativity which keeps us rebuilding the castle.*

Ainsley, do I ever blow up your castle?

Ainsley: No.

Anthony: *Why not? I try to, how come it never happens? Do you always defeat me?*

Ainsley: Yes.

Anthony: *In fact, don't you have a vehicle that fires darts and harpoons at my castle?*

Ainsley: You mean missiles

Anthony: *Oh, missiles. Yes. What are on the missiles that captured my bad guys?*

Ainsley: A net.

Anthony: *That's so crazy. How can that be? Do I ever win a battle?*

Ainsley: No

Anthony: *Sometimes in life, we don't win every battle we engage in. Sometimes it takes a superhero effort as leaders, to overcome those villains in life. Ainsley, when you're out with your girlfriends in the neighborhood? What do you and your girlfriends play with?*

Ainsley: We sometimes play in my pool. Sometimes we play on the trampoline.

Anthony: *Trampolines are fun. What about your crazy dogs Sparky and Bentley? Do they ever go into the pool?*

Ainsley: Bentley has gone in the pool once, but it looks like he has a tutu on when he's in the pool

Anthony: *His fur turns into a tutu? What a crazy thing. Well, you*

know, sometimes we have to jump into the deep end of the pool ourselves in life. I want you to think about four things:

When the sand castle doesn't come out of the mold the way you want it too, or the waves start to come up, what will you do?

What will you do if someone attacks your castle and knocks it down?

Do you attack it as an adult with systems and tasks? Or do you attack it like a child, who is an invincible superhero? You never lose a battle when you're a superhero and our best lessons are learned with those whom we play with as children.

Ainsley, do you like to play outside on a bike?

Ainsley: Yes, I'm good on my bike.

Anthony: *Excellent.*

I had a guest on the show recently, Jennifer Walsh, and she does a powerful podcast and show with guests in Central Park, New York City. I've listened to her become such a believer in the fact that when we are outside, it engages our creativity. It gives us a restful peace of mind to carry on. Think about children who play outside.

Are we spending any time outside relaxing and creating because the inside environment makes us more stagnant? Ainsley Jane from Florida has never seen a New Jersey boardwalk beach. Is that correct?

Ainsley: No. Never saw one.

Anthony: *We are going to go to the Jersey boardwalk because the boardwalk in New Jersey has everything you need for leadership and business. It has entertainment, it has challenges, commerce, it has all kinds of different things you can see to stimulate the mind. Today, Ainsley and I are going to go on a business retreat to the New Jersey boardwalk.*

The last thing I want to do as we wrap up the podcast today is ask you Ainsley, do you ever receive letters from Wolvie at your house in Florida? Do I ever write you letters or postcards?

Ainsley: You do, but I don't get them. Sometimes I don't get anything in the mail.

Anthony: *Well I'll have to start writing more letters to you. Where do you put the letters I send you?*

Ainsley: In the Wolvie box. It's nice and there is stuff that comes in the letters too.

Anthony: *I challenge you to think of something like this for yourself.*

It doesn't matter if you have grandchildren or not. It doesn't matter if you have children or not. What matters is that you use the power of letter writing to someone to encourage them, motivate them, inspire them and tell your story. Ainsley, do you like to play with doll babies? Who is your favorite doll?

Ainsley: Yes, Cry Baby.

Anthony: *I know Cry Baby has traveled all over the world, because you took her to Europe with you, your Mom and Dad for a month. How many countries did you go to?*

Ainsley: Six.

Anthony: *Wow. six countries. You went to visit your dad's family in the Czech Republic.*

Ainsley: And they have a dog.

Anthony: *They have a dog? What's the dog's name?*

Ainsley: Bentinka

Anthony: *Bentinka. That's a beautiful name. I was thinking about this when she was in Europe for a month and traveling six countries. As adults, we have to travel, maybe not physically, but we have to travel mentally.*

As we wrap up today, engage your childlike nature. Get outside and create. Look at life's challenges like a sandcastle. Sometimes you must build a moat to keep going and sometimes you have to ward off the villains who are trying to catch you with nets and missiles. Remember, it is the child within us who helps the adult become successful.

Ainsley, I love you. Thanks for helping Wolvie today. Everyone have a great day and thank you for listening.

The Child
Within

A leader's success should be based on the outcome of how they helped others.

We all have reasons for working hard and Pushing the Possible. For many of us, providing for family is the main reason we go to work and make money, however, in the day-to-day of providing for our families we get tired, run down, and overwhelmed by the tasks and forget why we push every day.

The demands of our spouses, our children, and our parents can become burdens we resent instead of it being a privilege to serve the ones we love. Marriages and families may break apart when these tasks become a weight and the joy is leached from our relationships. In today's world where both parents work, where kids spend much of their weekdays in daycare or school, and we strive to fill every minute of every day with tasks, extra-curricular activities, and technology, we risk losing our reason for pushing forward.

In a world where divorce is the norm and children are being raised by technology, as leaders we need to commit ourselves to being connected with those whom we love. No one person in a family is more important than the other, everyone needs to work together for the good of the family by finding ways to support one another. Building a strong family takes work, commitment, time, and is the most important thing we will ever do because our close relationships will enable us to make the impossible - possible.

What Ainsley Taught Us

Spend time with those who are important to you. Children can help us to find our inner child so we can play, imagine, and create. They remind us that we are born with the determination to work through frustrating problems by continuing to try until we master a skill. They can inspire us to be superheroes and fight the villains, even when it looks like we are going to lose.

Our children have so much to teach us, remind us of, and give us, however, in today's technological world we forget to give those whom we love the most valuable commodity we have, our full attention. We need to take the time to put away the distractions so we can receive their gifts. Time with our children is short, it goes by in an instant and if we value close family relationships, we need to step up and connect with them even if we are thousands of miles apart. Do not underestimate the importance of communication, no matter the tool used, to foster connection when you cannot be there with those whom you love.

Build deeper connections so we focus on each other in the real world.

Virtual connections are cemented with real world encounters and this is when opportunity shows up.

The Child Within

We must never lose the child within us. Successful leaders have an inner child who prevents them from being complacent. They are always at play, changing the rules to fit their next challenge. In every overachiever, you see the eyes of a playful child with the intensity of a focused professional.

We should all view photos of ourselves at different ages. Try placing the photographs in front of you starting from the youngest age to the most current year. Look at your eyes. Do they still have the fire and desire to play? Our eyes, it has been said, are the windows to our soul. Whether we are parents or business leaders, together we should build the playground of life. The playground is always open to these children of challenge to play and achieve their goals.

Children will always play with other children regardless of race or religion. If a child can look into our eyes and see another child, they will always follow us to their goals and dreams. After all is said and done, isn't life just a game? And who better to play a game than a leader with the spirit of a child.

Children are often fearless. They try different things because they believe they can accomplish every goal they attempt. They look at pessimists with a strange and confused look. They wonder why someone would speak of defeat prior to the start of the game. We hear people talk about adults as role models for children. Perhaps, children can serve as role models for adults.

The eyes of a child are the message center to the soul of achievement. Enjoy the game and never regret the result. Continue to seek new playmates who possess the drive and determination to never take you or themselves too seriously.

The Purpose of Life

When my father was suffering with ALS, people remembered the way he was before the illness; as kind hearted, a welder, a hard worker, and a good family man.

The purpose of life cannot be determined until we come to the end of it because it is based on how we impact the lives of others and how we are remembered. When people think about their time with us, they will remember the lessons, the humor, and the help we gave them during their weakest moments.

The podcast with my granddaughter was powerful for me because I saw the brilliance in her innocence. Perhaps our purpose in life is to remain innocent throughout it.

Do not be caustic. Do not be shallow, jilted, or biased. Be innocent. Be loving. Be the best you can be.

Push Your Possible

The Child Within

This is the part of the book where you dive deeply into the concepts to form your own opinions, make plans, and set goals.

I encourage you to mark up the pages and make this book a resource for your life journey.

Want to share your thoughts with me on social media? Tag me in your Twitter or LinkedIn post and use the hashtag, #PushersofPossible.

Childhood

Make a list of the things you did as a child which you do not do now. Why was it easier to 'Play' as a kid?

Childhood

What kind of child were you? Did you have lots of friends to play with or were you reading a book in your room? Explore how the adult you became is different from the child you were.

Responsibility

Your spouse, partner and/or family rely on you for certain responsibilities. Make a list of your responsibilities.

Connection

How will you meet all of your responsibilities, stay connected to friends and family, while pursuing your dream? Journal about how you feel, what thoughts you have, and why you believe you can succeed.

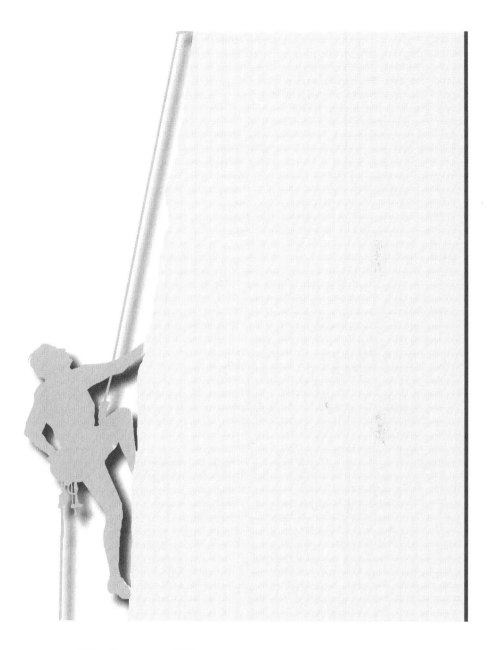

Six Degrees
of Impact

*Every day, mentors
are influenced
by their desire to
acquire new skills
and achieve peak
performance.
The best mentors
we know never
stop mentoring
themselves.*

As the CEO for the Marsh & McLennan Agency Northeast, and now Marsh Commercial, UK, people often asked me to define the role of a CEO. They want me to talk in terms of a Chief Executive Officer. But I'd rather not because honestly, I don't know how to define it or what it really means.

I do believe that everyone is a CEO.

I look at it this way, if you can coach yourself and others, can be entrepreneurial in your thinking, and act like an owner, you are a CEO, no matter your job or your title.

Nobody wakes up in the morning and thinks, "Let me look at the corporate organizational chart, I only have 4000 spaces to climb to become the CEO." Not a very motivating thought, is it? Wouldn't it be more motivating to see yourself as the head of your own company, right now, today?

I ask my colleagues to think of themselves as a CEO, because it is how I see them, and it is how I'd like you to see yourself. Imagine how different, how productive, how animated, how energetic you could be if your title, right now, was a CEO.

Imagine if we thought and acted like the CEO of our position in our family, our life, our business and our community? Imagine all of us thinking and acting like owners of everything we do.

Greatness is...

Think about how many times you have heard the word 'Great.' Great athlete. Great businessperson. Great celebrity. What does that mean? How do you define greatness?

Are we great when we hit every benchmark, every goal, every objective? Does the eight-year-old with straight A's come home and say, "I'm Great," and his parents say, "Yep, you are Great, you have made it, and now you are done?" Or is the CEO Great once they've hit their forecast for that quarter? Or they've hit their annual goals? Are they Great then?

I don't think hitting benchmarks is Greatness.

Perhaps the pinnacle of Greatness is when people duplicate what we did and continue what we started. Maybe then we are Great. I think that's a better definition. When my father, who was a role model passed away from ALS, he asked me to duplicate what he started so it could continue for the family. He'd built a supportive family dynamic and I was honored to continue his legacy as a leader who helped others.

Are you improving the quality of life for your family and loved ones? Are you improving the quality of life for the people whom you work with and serve? Are people happy to come into an environment where you lead, or do they feel it's something they have to do to earn compensation?

Success will never be achieved until people seek to duplicate what you started.

The Six Degrees Model

I wrote a book years ago with a woman named Monique ter Haar called *Six Degrees of Impact*, which is an organizational development model I have used to turn organizations around and help them to Push toward their Possible. At Marsh & McLennan Northeast, the Six Degrees model helped the team Push to their Possible and it continues to push them forward after I left to lead the Marsh Commercial team in the UK, where I am also implementing this model.

The next few pages will ask questions to help you create Six Degrees of Impact for yourself. For a more in depth look at each degree, the book *Six Degrees of Impact* is available on Amazon.

Bringing it all Together

As you answer the questions on the following pages, bring what you have discovered in previous pages to create a plan of action to help you achieve your Possible. This will give you a chance to clarify your answers, to communicate to your support system, and to develop a strong foundation upon which to build.

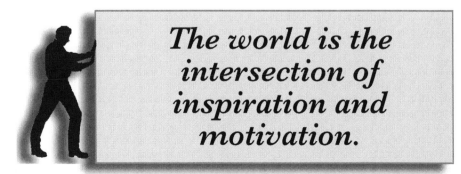

The world is the intersection of inspiration and motivation.

Six Degrees of Impact

The first degree in the Six Degrees of Impact is **Leadership**. Describe your current leadership style. What are the strengths and weaknesses in your style?

Define the servant leadership style in your own words. What behavioural indicators do all servant leaders exhibit?

Identify the gaps between your current leadership style and the servant leadership style. How will you fill those gaps?

The next degree in the model is **Marketing** and I don't mean in terms of commercial sense. The next step is how you tell your personal story, your personal brand.

What are your core values?

Define your personal mission statement and personal vision statement.

Step three is determining what **Resources** you need to be successful and make constant improvements in self-development.

What self-improvement resources do you need?

What support do you need from your family and friends?

What opportunities are there in your community to help you network with other people and expand your personal brand message?

The fourth degree is **Strategic Positon**. Change is for everyone and happens because of outside factors and influences. What I am asking you to do is think about evolving. How will you evolve to your Pinnacle of Greatness to move from where you are today to where you want to be?

How will you act like a CEO and own your position?

The next degree is **Research Development**. Leaders are lifelong learners because they know they need to keep evolving and pushing toward the next Possible. Whether it is learning a new language or moving to a different department within your organization, you have to put yourself into research and development mode.

Which topics do you want to research and how do these topics help you reach your Pinnacle of Greatness?

The last degree is **Outcomes**. What final outcome are you trying to achieve?

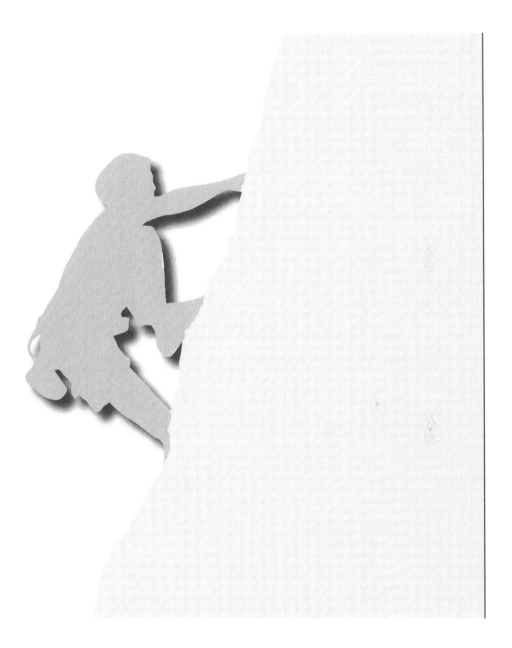

Goals and Support

Are You in your Own Way?

Long before becoming the CEO of the Marsh & McLennan Agency in the Northeast, I sometimes struggled with focus, discipline, and all the issues many of us encounter. But I knew I had to do more than change my job title to obtain the life I wanted for myself.

I had to ask myself some hard questions and find the courage to answer them honestly because lying was not going to help me move in the right direction. I developed a Personal Strategic Plan to help me discover the answers.

When you match your goals to what you're trying to do in your life, your profession, and your job, happiness will ensue.

Are your Goals Equal to your Potential?

Often times, we struggle with welding our passion to our potential to increase our performance. As you define your short and long-term goals, think about welding them to your potential.

In the past, I used overview goals to formulate my mission, to be a welcome leader in any arena I chose to stand in. As time went on, I realized in my life, both personally and professionally, the goals had to be more specific.

For a dream to become a goal you need to write it down, give yourself a deadline, and outline a metric you will use to measure your success.

"Dreams are Goals with Deadlines."

The goal process should never be taken lightly; it is not one of those measures that becomes commonplace. Cheating on your goal is similar to robbing your heritage and desecrating the foundation of the overachiever who came before you. Leaders are not like everyone else who plays the game. Leaders are the creators and visionaries of the goals of others. If we take our goals lightly, we short-arm the future for those whom we lead. Every moment we fail to support each other and second-guess our achievement, we prevent the survival and success of the system. No matter where we go, goals follow us and bang loudly on our souls. In the end, it was never the goals that drove us; it was always the need, desire, and courage to conquer them. To take them lightly is to assume we were never here at all.

Goals create the future of an organization and the well-being of a family. We cannot count on someone else to deliver our future and dream our dreams for us. We can set examples for our families and all those who follow in our steps. We have no right to question the goals of our children if we constantly fall short of our own goals.

Goals are the internal energy propelling a professional to success.

We might only have six minutes to get a goal accomplished, as there may be no long-term opportunity. Short-term is nothing more than putting some kind of a quantifier on the goal to complete it in a realistically fast period of time. Long-term is a vision of the future built on a foundation of successful short-term goals.

Together, we can strive to reach heights which seemed too high for us. Discussing our goals with others is one of the most successful ways of dealing with achievement and staying focused. Tell people what you are trying to accomplish because it puts a subtle pressure on us to deliver upon our goal. It also helps people point us in the right direction. It is critical we follow through using direct action to take steps to continue forward because we do not want to process items repeatedly like a hamster on a wheel.

Planning is the glue to our goal process. Our goals are brought to conclusion through thoughtful processes. Remember, although we have to be successful at what we create, we also want to challenge ourselves to be better than our current selves. It is important we set short and long-term goals which challenge us. I have found that what stops most people from achieving success is their inability to change and try new endeavors. Goals force us to stretch and to achieve in areas where we have not yet been successful, may be uncomfortable, or we have not attempted to penetrate in the past. We have to put in the effort to plan, to look at short-term and long-term goals, measure and have the ability to change or pivot.

A Team is a Force of One

So much has been written about goal setting and how critical it is for organizations and individuals to set goals, yet rarely are we clear on how to implement or communicate the goal process. As I discussed before, visualization is critical in goal planning. The process is easier than you think. With the help of the exercises in this book, identify and build on your strengths, both personally and professionally. You will then able to project how things will look in the future based on those same strengths. It is not necessary to abandon your current delivery system, but merely expand upon it. Based on your current planning and goal-setting methods, you can project what the environment will look like in the future.

If people do not believe in the dream and vision of the company, they will not follow the goal-setting process in the future. To combat apathy within the company, leadership must give people the chance to debate and discuss the vision. This process will help them to support the company's entrepreneurial spirit because they were involved in the goal planning process and can attach themselves to leadership's vision and dream. As they watch leadership planning well into the future, they may feel compelled to plan for their own futures by creating individual goals.

I have found few individuals can really plan for the future and build their own perpetuation plans. Many speak of it, but few can truly deliver a solid functional plan. Part of the planning process and part of the goal-setting environment is to decide early on whom you will collaborate with to accomplish your tasks. At our organization, we have colleagues who are driven and dedicated. Even though they may lack the overall picture of the entire company, they know the goals and leader's vision, so can focus on their particular area of expertise. Without them, the delivery system would fail, but with them change and creativity is common and cherished. Many people are surprised when they fail at accomplishing goals or fail to achieve their level of goal-setting processes because there are some external or internal reasons which caused the process to break down. They may have relied solely on their ability and instinct which may be sufficient in a short-term goal process, but inappropriate for the long-term. Certainly, as we get older, we realize the need to have creative talent around us in order to support our long-range planning process. If not, it's no different than being on a construction site and having the most high-powered equipment tunnel trenches that then collapse. The tunneling process goes very quickly, but when the machinery stops and you turn around, you notice everything disintegrated because no one had been laying pipe and back-filling the ditch. Conclusion: we realize planning and goal setting go hand in hand.

Supporting Those who Support You

Where can you find the people to fill your team? By getting to know the people with whom you work. If as a leader you hold yourself above everyone else and are too far removed from them, you will miss finding emerging leaders.

Take Kim, who worked closely with me on the Roots of Leadership Podcast. When I met her she was the receptionist at Marsh & McLennan Northeast. If I'd ignored her as insignificant to my responsibilities, I never would have discovered her talent and passion for writing. She now works in the creative relations department and does a remarkable job with the podcast.

Or Caryn Ojeda, when I met Caryn, she was doing project work for us on seminar systems and now she is the producer of the Roots of Leadership Podcast and helping with branding for individuals and companies. She is fantastic at what she does.

Each of these women supported me and in turn, I support them in their careers. I would not have known what they were capable of, what they wanted to do, and what was possible, if I had walked past them every day with my nose in the air because my ego says "I'm the all-important CEO." No. My job as CEO is to bring the right resources into the organization to help it grow, to coach the people I am responsible for, and motivate everyone to be the best they can be every day. When I am doing my job correctly, I find the people whom I need on teams throughout the company to support the long-term goals.

Success does not come from one individual doing everything or dictating what is to be done. It comes when everyone passionately makes the effort to move together as one toward set goals. As a result of my consistently supporting my teams, nurturing, and working with them, there has always more than one person who can step into my position when I vacate it. I believe that when you build a strong, passionate team, it should work this way. Promotion from within could not have happened if I had walled myself off in an ivory tower and had not supported and collaborated with the people who make up my teams.

Is Your Next Step, the Right Step?

Who are the people you surround yourself with? Who are the people who support you, who can help you plan your next step and tie it back to your Personal Strategic Plan? Do you have a Personal Board of Directors? Did you do the work and create the list of those whom you want to sit on your board? Were there names you forgot to add? Go back to your list, firm it up, and ask them to help you write your Personal Strategic Plan and hold you accountable to your goals.

A Living Document

I wrote my first book, *Creating Reality*, almost 20 years ago and when I reread it now, much of the perspective is not the same, because the passion, the goals, the dreams, and the aspirations have been changed. The Personal Strategic Plan which I'm asking you to build is a living document that will continue to evolve as you do. As you become more courageous and confident, as you begin to surround yourself with people who think the same way, your life will change.

You have what it takes to do this.

You do not have to be in the front to lead. You can be in any position to lead. You can lead from the rear. I've met people of all ages who have the power, the energy, the mindset, the tenacity, and the focus to achieve.
In my life, every time I tried something new, I've encountered

people who believed it couldn't be done. People close to me said I couldn't go from working construction to an office. Then when I was working in the insurance business and I started to write books, people said I couldn't do that. Every time I took on a new venture that looked to be outside of where others believed I should be, I met detractors, as you will, but they don't matter. What matters is how you see yourself, the dreams you have, and the people you surround yourself with. Who will support you?

What Moments will You Make?

Think about your day, your week, your month, your year? What moments are you seeking to create? Make as many moments and opportunities for yourself, those you love, and those your serve.

What Seems Impossible to Achieve?

As you put your strategic plan into action, as you connect it to a goal and objective, an action and a strategy, as you assign times and structure, and as you select people who will help you, what you believed is impossible, will become reality.

> *Whatever I am doing, I am always also learning something else. When I was an insurance professional, I started to think about consultation, risk management, writing books & doing podcasts, all while being the best at what I was doing at the time.*

Push Your Possible

Goals and Support

This is the part of the book where you dive deeply into the concepts to form your own opinions, make plans, and set goals.

I encourage you to mark up the pages and make this book a resource for your life journey.

Want to share your thoughts with me on social media? Tag me in your Twitter or LinkedIn post and use the hashtag, #PushersofPossible.

Goals and Plans

Refer back to the dream you wrote when you started reading this book. It will take lots of goals for you to achieve your dream. Take a moment to write down some goals and how you will measure their successful completion. List the tasks which need to be completed to meet each goal.

What is your big scary goal?

What do you want to achieve in 10 years? Date: _____

What do you want to achieve in 5 years? Date: _____

What do you want to achieve in 2 years? Date: _____

What do you want to achieve in 1 year? Date: _____

What do you want to achieve in 6 months? Date:_____

What do you want to achieve in 1 month? Date:_____

What do you want to achieve this week? Date: _____

Goals and Plans

In order to achieve these goals you will need to accomplish small tasks on a regular basis, which will help you monitor your progress. List out the tasks and how frequently you will need to complete each task to ensure you are moving toward your goal. **Ex:** Write one Linkedin story a day.

Success

What does success look like to you? Go back to your Big Scary Dream at the beginning of this book. Picture yourself in the middle of it.

Who is with you in your Big Scary Dream?

What do you need to have to consider yourself successful? Is it money? Position? Family? Define what success looks like to you.

Who has the life you want and how is it different than yours?

In the future, living the dream, what will you able to do which you can't do today? What will success enable you to do for yourself and your family (people)?

Support

What does support look like to you? What do you want your family and friends to do when they are supporting you? What do you need?

What if they are unable to support you in the way you need them to? What will you do? Where else can you find support?

Supporting Others

While you are focused on Pushing your Possible, how can you support those whom you love as they Push for their Possible?

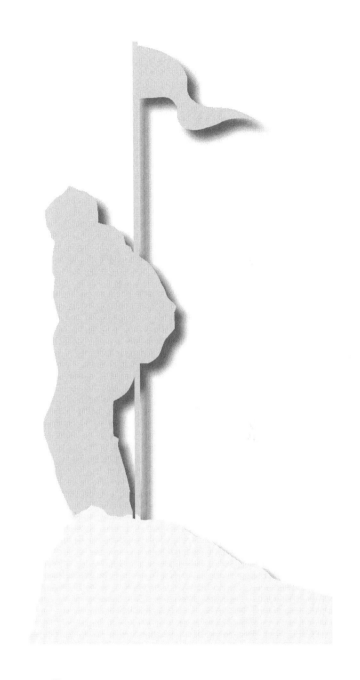

Reflection

*You can create
best practices for
achieving success in
your life. What are
you prepared to do to
ensure you stand on
the edge of greatness?*

This is Anthony Gruppo. I am coming up to the Roots of Leadership Podcast's first anniversary and I'd like to share with you some of the things we've learned from our guests and from you, our listeners.

When it comes to backgrounds and experiences, our guests have spanned the gamut. I have talked to leaders in private equity, community-based services, the arts, performance, coaching, life sciences, cosmetics, and staffing companies. All of my guests have had a major impact on me in areas I believed were platforms in my life; areas I had based a lot of my own decisions around.

The questions listeners have sent in have made me think a great deal about my personal strategic plan and belief system. I have received questions like, can that truly happen to me in my life? Do I have what it takes to become one of the individuals interviewed in the podcast? How do I deal with complacency, barriers, and the people who stand in the way to my Possible?

The perception might be, "I am not good enough."

We all have those gremlins nagging in the back of our minds, planting doubts. Even CEOs of large International Companies battle with self-doubt. How do we overcome the negative messages, which will determine if we are able to Push the Possible and climb our own ladders to success?

All of our guests are servant leaders. In this podcast we have explored what it means to be a servant leader, what it looks like and how it affects those whom we serve, no matter what position we are in. When we support and serve those whom support us, we build a community, not just a culture. By being part of the community, we find talented people who do amazing things to help a company grow.

I want to take a moment to thank our staff and specifically Caryn Ojeda, my producer for all her hard work and Kim Cummings, who writes the descriptions on the website. These individuals weren't in the media business a year ago, they were insurance and risk professionals who found the ability to learn to be successful in a new vocation entirely.

Learn from these wonderful ladies and ask yourself, which areas can you stretch yourself into? What is new, different, and a bit uncomfortable for you?

All of the guests on the show who became leaders in life and business did not start out on top. They jumped in, learned what they had to, did the work, and Pushed the Possible to the top.

Jennifer Davis and Elizabeth McCourt, spoke about how they found great success in the corporate world before leaving to start their own company. I think about people like Hakika, the youngest female franchisee, who took $500 and built a very successful business. Barry Beck made a million dollars before he graduated college by building a cleaning services maintenance company, before moving on to launch Bluemercury. Jennifer Walsh is an inspirational visionary who founded Beauty Bar, and is one of the top wellness professionals in the nation. Chris Sugden who through the power of persistence Pushed the Possible in the world of private equity. Guests like, Michelle Sartain, the head of United

States sales for Marsh, taught me to have a looser Personal Strategic Plan, so opportunities can find their way to me.

Then there is the podcast with the most downloads. The one closest to my heart; my interview with my granddaughter Ainsley Jane, who gave us a child's perspective of life because we do not want to lose our inner child.

Think for a Moment About You

Today's podcast is just you and me looking for the edge, which should make you a little uncomfortable.

I interviewed Dr. Laura Gallaher, the CEO of Galloper Edge, who at the age of 24 was asked by NASA to talk about the psychological issues of organizational leadership soon after the space shuttle Columbia was lost, killing all on board. At the age of 24, she was thrust to the edge of her risk tolerance and went on to be successful.

The people I interviewed weren't born with any special gift, which you do not have. They are just like you. Steve Maneri, who played for various NFL teams and was coached by some of the league's greats had a number of people competing for his position, forcing him to define his edge of risk.

Sarah Diane Post from Nebraska is a housewife, who after her fifth child and weighing 200 pounds went through a transformational evolution to remake herself. Although she battles anxiety, she was able to take control and now speaks to groups about transformational wellness. Perhaps you can identify with her struggle and transformation.

My Edge of Risk

I grew up in a blue-collar household; my father was a welder, and my mother was a sewing machine operator. There are a lot of times in my life when I felt it was good enough to take whatever job I could and do it for the rest of my life, day in and day out. I could have stayed in a comfortable place knowing I was good at what I did and didn't need to push myself to be other than where I started. I could have gone through life without growing, striving, or climbing the ladder of success. And most importantly, I could have remained far away from the edge of risk.

As I think back on my life, I realize how much danger I've put myself and my family in, as I pushed past the security of stability into the uncertainty of growth and change. There was a time in business when I was asked to take over a struggling enterprise in Texas. I remember it being so difficult when I first arrived, I began to plan my exit for when I failed. What struck me was, in the moment I began to think about my escape, I was doomed for failure. Once I changed my mindset and went on to helping the operations in Texas be successful, everything relaxed. I didn't worry about where I would go if I failed, I just knew what I would do when we succeeded.

Thanks to my colleagues in Texas, we turned it around.
I remember being asked to help organically grow an organization that was struggling in Erie Pennsylvania, which is a community of maybe three to four hundred thousand people. It was a

manufacturing city that had fallen on hard times. People didn't understand why I would risk my career by going where there was no chance of success. When I arrived there, I found amazing people, driven people, who are able to do more with less and with new concepts and innovations, we became successful.

Thank You

The Roots of Leadership Podcast is about helping you find your Possible because if you are willing to work hard, take risks, and get uncomfortable, you deserve to succeed.

Thank you so much for listening and supporting us with words of encouragement. Thank you to the guests who have come on our show. As no one man or woman builds anything successful on their own, you have helped me build this show.

You can defy the odds. You can define your way to greatness. There is a servant leader in all of you who can take rejection and move on. You can go one-on-one with some of the toughest individuals. As Karen Mayo said, there's a mindful science to learning. You can create transformational leadership for yourself. You can learn to be a force of one. You can live in the moment where you stand, and in that moment, you can create the best practices for achieving successful outcomes.

I remember Chantal Raineri, who after losing her father at a young age, swore she would never be dependent on anyone or any one thing again. She went on in her life to become one of the most successful businesswomen in our industry. She took tragedy to triumph and you can too.

There are many of you out there who have faced those moments, who have lost loved ones, lost a job, had to reinvent yourself, and had to deal with the care of an aging parent or taking care of children as a single parent. You don't make excuses for what happened. You are an individual of great courage.

Courage is founded in the uncomfortable.

I thank all our guests of the last year and all the listeners for making us better.

Don't back up. Don't retreat. Don't surround yourself with 'Yes' people who only tell you what you want to hear. Seek out the voices of the people who will challenge you to become a new and more courageous person in the future. We stand together on the platform of humanity. You are the difference makers. You are the news makers. You are a Pusher of the Possible.

This is Anthony Gruppo and thank you for being a part of my life.

Push Your Possible

Your Journal

This is the part of the book where you dive deeply into the concepts to form your own opinions, make plans, and set goals.

I encourage you to mark up the pages and make this book a resource for your life journey.

Want to share your thoughts with me on social media? Tag me in your Twitter or LinkedIn post and use the hashtag, #PushersofPossible.

Push Yourself

Make a list of things you fear, that might be holding you back from success. Then write down how you can push toward your Possible.

For example: **Fear:** Walking into a room full of new people
Push the Possible: Go to new networking meetings once a week and meet ten new people

Fear:

Push the Possible:

Fear:

Push the Possible:

Fear:

Push the Possible:

Fear:

Push the Possible:

Fear:

Push the Possible:

Fear:

Push the Possible:

Fear:

Push the Possible:

Fear:

Push the Possible:

Fear:

Push the Possible:

# Check in

Come back to this book once a month and see where you are in relation to where you were. Keep track of your progress to help you Push your Possible

Date:

Think about what you did over the last month. What worked and why?

Think about what you did over the last month. What did not work and why?

Date:

Think about what you did over the last month. What worked and why?

Think about what you did over the last month. What did not work and why?

Date:

What you did over the last month. What worked and why?

What you did over the last month. What did not work and why?

Date:

What you did over the last month. What worked and why?

What you did over the last month. What did not work and why?

Date:

What you did over the last month. What worked and why?

What you did over the last month. What did not work and why?

Date:

What you did over the last month. What worked and why?

What you did over the last month. What did not work and why?

Date:

What you did over the last month. What worked and why?

What you did over the last month. What did not work and why?

Date:

What you did over the last month. What worked and why?

What you did over the last month. What did not work and why?

Books by Anthony Gruppo
Available on Amazon

Creating Reality

This book was written to serve as a guide to develop the mindset necessary for achievement, providing insight to follow dreams and accomplish goals. Leadership, marketing and motivation are the keys to success in leading others. In "Creating Reality", Anthony shares with his readers the forces, experiences, lessons and individuals who shaped his life and helped make him successful. Let Anthony's road map of experience, vision and unique perspective give you the direction to "Create Reality".

Roots of Leadership - A Journal

The Roots of Leadership is a multifaceted journal that serves up a collection of original inspirational quotes spanning key life topics, from career and personal strategic planning, family and fellowship to self-reflection and individual-optimization.

This journal's unique offering is that it enables you to deep dive into the quotes, many of which have accompanying self-reflective action items, designed to enhance their impact and create lasting, supportive outcomes. No matter where you are in your life's journey, this journal can act as a catalyst for personal change and evolution. Journaling is a practice with a long history and is shown to provide a host of benefits from stress management and improved self-discipline to increased awareness and tapping into spirituality. *The Roots of Leadership Journal* has the added benefit of providing you with personal guidance.

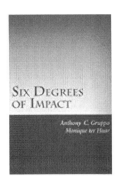

Six Degrees of Impact

Six Degrees of Impact: Breaking Corporate Glass provides perspectives and strategies for leading an environment toward positive change. We all have a voice in how our environment evolves. *Six Degrees of Impact* is like having a consultant in the palm of your hand. This book provides you with short stories for each of the Degrees which are the keys to integrated change management. The Six Degrees framework is built upon leadership, strategic positioning, research & development, marketing, resources and outcomes.

Six Degrees Journal

Journal your personal path to greatness using the Six Degrees prompts of personal leadership development. This innovative journal helps you to build a personal strategic plan and contains original motivational quotes by the author of *Six Degrees of Impact.*

Under Construction

Everyone is constantly under construction. This book provides the reader with thoughts and concepts for constructing their success. *Under Construction* is a coalescing of experiences to guide you toward maximizing and leveraging your personal potential and abilities.

NOTES

Dear Reader,

Thank you for purchasing this copy of Pushers of the Possible. We would love to get your feedback through online reviews and social media. Please use the hashtag #PushersofPossible. We look forward to sharing your journey to possible.

The Pushers of the Possible Team

NOTES

YOUR THOUGHTS

NOTES

FAVOURITE QUOTES

NOTES

IDEAS

NOTES

Printed in Poland
by Amazon Fulfillment
Poland Sp. z o.o., Wrocław